Penn Greek Drama Series

Series Editors
David R. Slavitt
Palmer Bovie

The Penn Greek Drama Series presents fresh literary translations of the entire corpus of classical Greek drama: tragedies, comedies, and satyr plays. The only contemporary series of all the surviving work of Aeschylus, Sophocles, Euripides, Aristophanes, and Menander, this collection brings together men and women of literary distinction whose versions of the plays in contemporary English poetry can be acted on the stage or in the individual reader's theater of the mind.

The aim of the series is to make this cultural treasure accessible, restoring as faithfully as possible the original luster of the plays and offering in living verse a view of what talented contemporary poets have seen in their readings of these works so fundamental a part of Western civilization.

Sophocles, 2

King Oedipus, Oedipus at Colonus, Antigone

Edited by
David R. Slavitt *a n d* Palmer Bovie

PENN

University of Pennsylvania Press
Philadelphia

10 9 8 7 6 5 4 3 2 1

Published by
University of Pennsylvania Press
Philadelphia, Pennsylvania 19104-4011

Library of Congress Cataloging-in-Publication Data
Sophocles
    [Works. English. 1998]
    Sophocles / edited by David R. Slavitt and Palmer Bovie
      p.   cm. — (Penn Greek drama series)
      Contents: 1. Ajax. Women of Trachis. Philoctetes. — 2. King Oedipus.
Oedipus at Colonus. Antigone.
      ISBN 0-8122-3445-6 (v. 1: cloth : alk. paper). —ISBN 0-8122-1653-9
    (v. 1: pbk : alk. paper). —ISBN 0-8122-3462-6 (v. 2: cloth : alk. paper).—
    ISBN 0-8122-1666-0 (v. 2: pbk : alk. paper)
      1. Sophocles—Translations into English.   2. Greek drama (Tragedy)—
    Translations into English.   3. Mythology (Greek)—Drama.   I. Slavitt,
    David R., 1935–   .   II. Bovie, Smith Palmer.   III. Title.   IV. Series.
    PA4414.A2   1998
    882′.01—DC21   98-9962
                                                                       CIP

Contents

Introduction

Palmer Bovie

Classical Greek tragedy, which flourished in Athens during the fifth century B.C., grew out of country festivals originating a century earlier. Three different celebrations in honor of Dionysus, known as the rural Dionysia, occurred during the winter months. One of these, the Lenaea, was also observed at Athens in the sanctuary of Dionysus. In addition to song it offered ecstatic dances and comedy. Another, the Anthesteria, lasted for three days as a carnival time of revelry and wine drinking. It also included a remembrance of the dead and was believed to be connected with Orestes' mythical return to Athens purged of guilt for killing his mother Clytemnestra.

The rural Dionysia were communal holidays observed to honor Dionysus, the god of wine, of growth and fertility, and of lightning. Free-spirited processions to an altar of Dionysus were crowned by lyrical odes to the god sung by large choruses of men and boys chanting responsively under the direction of their leader. The ritual included the sacrifice of a goat at the god's altar, from which the term "tragedy," meaning goat-song, may derive. Gradually themes of a more serious nature gained ground over the joyful, exuberant addresses to the liberating god, legends of familiar heroes, and mythological tales of divine retribution. But the undercurrent of the driving Dionysiac spirit was seldom absent, even in the sophisticated artistry of the masterful tragic poets of the fifth century.

Initially the musical texts were antiphonal exchanges between the chorus and its leader. Thespis, who won the prize of a goat for tragedy at Athens in 534 B.C., is traditionally said to have been the first to appear as an actor, separate from the chorus, speaking a prologue and making set speeches, with his face variously disguised by a linen mask. A fourth festival, the City Dionysia or the Great Dionysia, was instituted by the ruler Peisistratus, also in 534, and nine years later Aeschylus was born. It seems that the major era of Greek tragic art was destined to begin.

The Great Dionysia, an annual occasion for dramatic competitions in tragedy and comedy, was held in honor of Dionysus Eleutheros. Its five-day celebration began with a procession in which the statue of Dionysus was carried to the nearby village of Eleutherai (the site of the Eleusinian Mysteries) and then back, in a parade by torchlight, to Athens and the precincts of Dionysus on the lower slopes of the Acropolis. In the processional ranks were city officials, young men of military age leading a bull, foreign residents of Athens wearing scarlet robes, and participants in the dramatic contests, including the producers (*choregoi*), resplendent in colorful costumes. The ceremonies ended with the sacrificial slaughter of the bull and the installation of Dionysus' statue on his altar at the center of the orchestra.

For three days each of the poets chosen for the competition presented his work, three tragedies and one satyr play (a farcical comedy performed in the afternoon after an interval following the staging of tragedies). In the late afternoon comedies were offered. The other two days were marked by dithyrambic competitions, five boys' choruses on one day, five men's on the other. The dithyramb, earlier an excited dramatic dance, became in the Athenian phase a quieter performance, sung by a chorus of fifty and offering little movement.

The theater of Dionysus at Athens was an outdoor space on the southern slope of the Acropolis. A semicircular auditorium was created on the hillside from stone or marble slabs, or shaped from the natural rock with wooden seats added. Narrow stepways gave access to the seats, the front row of which could be fitted out with marble chairs for official or distinguished members of the audience. From sites visible today at Athens, Delphi, Epidaurus, and elsewhere, it is evident that the sloping amphitheater had excellent acoustic properties and that the voices of the actors and the chorus were readily heard.

The acting area began with an *orchestra*, a circular space some sixty feet in diameter where the chorus performed its dance movements, voiced its commentaries, and engaged in dialogue with the actors. In the center of the orchestra was an altar of Dionysus, and on it a statue of the god. Behind the orchestra several steps led to a stage platform in front of the *skene*, a wooden building with a central door and doors at each end and a flat roof. The actors could enter and exit through these doors or one of the sides, retiring to assume different masks and costumes for a change of role. They could also appear on the roof for special effects, as in Euripides' *Orestes* where at the end Orestes and Pylades appear, menacing Helen with death, before she is whisked away from them by Apollo. The skene's facade represented a palace or temple and could have an altar in front of it. Stage properties included the *eccyclema*, a wheeled platform that was rolled out from the central door or the side of the skene to display an interior setting or a tableau, as at the end of Aeschylus' *Agamemnon* where the murdered bodies of Agamemnon and Cassandra are proudly displayed by Clytemnestra.

Another piece of equipment occasionally brought into play was the *mechane*, a tall crane that could lift an actor or heavy objects (e.g., Medea in her chariot) high above the principals' heads. This device, also known as the *deus ex machina*, was favored by Euripides who, in the climactic scene of *Orestes* shows Apollo protecting Helen in the air high above Orestes and Pylades on the roof. Or a deity may appear above the stage to resolve a final conflict and bring the plot to a successful conclusion, as the figure of Athena does at the end of Euripides' *Iphigenia in Tauris*. Sections of background at each end of the stage could be revolved to indicate a change of scene. These *periaktoi*, triangular in shape, could be shown to the audience to indicate a change of place or, together with thunder and lightning machines, could announce the appearance of a god.

The actors wore masks that characterized their roles and could be changed offstage to allow one person to play several different parts in the same drama. In the earliest period tragedy was performed by only one actor in counterpoint with the chorus, as could be managed, for example, in Aeschylus' *Suppliants*. But Aeschylus himself introduced the role of a second actor, simultaneously present on the stage, Sophocles made use of a third, and he and Euripides probably a fourth. From such simple elements (the orchestra space for the chorus, the slightly raised stage and its scene front, the minimal cast of actors) was created the astonishingly powerful poetic drama of the fifth-century Athenian poets.

What we can read and see today is but a small fraction of the work produced by the three major poets and a host of fellow artists who presented plays in the dramatic competitions. Texts of tragedies of Aeschylus, Sophocles, and Euripides were copied and stored in public archives at Athens, along with Aristophanes' comedies. At some later point a selection was made of the surviving plays, seven by Aeschylus, seven by Sophocles, nine by Euripides, and ten others of his discovered by chance. In the late third and early second centuries B.C., this collection of thirty-three plays was conveyed to the great library of Alexandria, where scholarly commentaries, *scholia*, formed part of the canon, to be copied and transmitted to students and readers in the Greco-Roman cultural world.

Sophocles (496–406 B.C.) was born at Colonus and lived as one of Athens' most admired artists and respected public citizens during the era of the city's prosperity, cultural glory, imperial expansion, and disastrous struggle against Sparta in the Peloponnesian War. In 443 he was elected imperial treasurer; he was elected general at least twice, once as a colleague of Pericles and later serving with Nicias after the Sicilian expedition. Among his friends were the philosopher Archelaus and the artist Polygnotus, who painted a portrait of Sophocles in the Stoa holding a lyre. He was a priest of the healing deity Alcon and made his own house a temporary place of worship of Asclepius until his temple was ready. In recognition of this reverential tribute Sophocles was honored as a hero after his death and awarded the title *Dexion*. A few months before his death he appeared with his chorus, dressed in black, in mourning for Euripides at the preliminary to the Great Dionysia. Such a generous public gesture well illustrates the noble character of his long-lived creative spirit.

Sophoclean technique differs from Aeschylean. Sophocles increased the number of chorus members to fifteen, from Aeschylus' twelve. The role of the chorus is, however, less closely attached to the actors' predicament; instead, the choral odes stand out in their lustrous lyrics as complementary interludes expressing themes of confidence and exaltation on the brink of a grim development in the plot. Or in colorful imagery they trace the contours of a landscape animate with natural beauty; or compare a corner of the world of myth that bears on a situation in the drama. Like the sayings of an Aeschylean chorus, Sophocles' stage groups proffer somber advice or deplore the sinister turn of events.

In structure and style Sophocles advances the pace and clarity of action far beyond Aeschylus' crushing pageants of power. By introducing the third actor he gains more play in the thrust and counterthrust of dialogue. Electra can involve her sister Chrysothemis in the plan to destroy Clytemnestra; and when Chrysothemis argues for the preferable course of compromise,

Orestes come into play as the avenging agent. Antigone contends with her sister Ismene as well as with Creon; the latter's son, Haemon, adds to the interlocking tensions by opposing his father's sentence against Antigone. In *Oedipus at Colonus* five different figures vie for Oedipus' good will—Antigone and Ismene, their brother Polynices, Creon, and Theseus—but the dominant personality of the aged Oedipus prevails in scene after scene, strong-minded and endowed with the mysterious power to confer blessings on the land of Athens.

Abandoning the trilogy, Sophocles studies related themes in different lights: *King Oedipus* was produced some fifteen years after *Antigone*, presented in 441 B.C. when Sophocles was fifty-four; *Oedipus at Colonus* was first produced in 405, the year after his death at the age of ninety. Among his voluminous output of some 123 tragedies, Sophocles' recurrent interest in the fascinating myth of the Theban dynasty displays a masterful treatment of this complex narrative. *King Oedipus* delineates the classical model of the tragic hero, an admirable figure who, because of some flaw in character, mistakes his aim (*hamartia*) and undergoes a reversal of situation (*peripeteia*), which causes his downfall in such a spectacular manner as to evoke the combined feelings of pity and fear in the minds of the spectators. These were the terms applied by Aristotle in his fourth-century critique, the *Poetics*. Aristotle considered Sophocles' art to be a perfection of form, and certainly his judgment applies to *King Oedipus*. As the hero moves forward step by step in his investigation of the identity of the person responsible for the calamitous situation of Thebes, he gains his first insight into the possibility of his own involvement, at the center of the drama, where he first experiences a "wandering of the mind" on being told that Laius was murdered "at the crossing of three roads." Oedipus remembers that he himself had killed a man at such a place. From this point on, every new message intended as a reassuring piece of information becomes, ironically, one more bit of damaging evidence in the case against Oedipus himself, the misguided perpetrator of an unspeakable crime. Far different from the proud "tyrant," the ruler who at the beginning of his inquiry defiantly withstood the warnings of Creon and Tiresias and the concerns of his wife, Jocasta, Oedipus, the abject victim of his own obstinate intellect, has discovered the truth. It reduces him to fathomless sorrow and the frenzied violence of self-mutilation. He gouges out the eyes that have looked into the heart of the matter.

In legend, as *Oedipus at Colonus* shows, the hero, although brought to a wretched state of existence, blind and bedraggled, dependent on Antigone's arm for guidance, is not destroyed by his innocent plunge into criminal behavior. He has, rather, become schooled by his phenomenal suffering and ultimately purified; graced with an aura of sanctity, he has acquired a mysterious power, associated with the virtuous will of the Eumenides. He exerts this redeemed power in the form of a blessing on Athens and its civic ideals under the leadership of Theseus, and vanishes into eternal life as a spiritual force for good.

The stalwart contenders in *Antigone* experience no such redemption but meet their fate in grim reality. The double dénouement carries the three principals briskly forward to disaster. Antigone confronts Creon, maintaining in ferociously brilliant terms the superiority of religious principles to Creon's blasphemous edict that Polynices' body be left to rot exposed and unburied. When Antigone is found to have defied the ruler's sacrilegious order by performing symbolic burial rites for her brother, she is sentenced to death by starvation in a rock-walled cave. Creon is then confronted by his son Haemon, the heroine's intended husband: the young man, outraged by his father's cruelty and pride, vows never to see him again and rushes away to try to save Antigone from her fate. Creon's next antagonist is the blind seer Tiresias, who pronounces stern warnings against Creon's misguided punishment of the maiden for her piety. Creon angrily accuses the soothsayer of mercenary motives, of "propheteering" by foretelling the future fraudulently. He stands at the summit of his hubris, the arrogant pride that has led him implacably from one error in judgment to another. The chorus of citizens now intervenes with Creon, urging him to relent, and he suddenly sees the wisdom of refraining from violence. He goes to Antigone's cave to release her. She has already found release in death by hanging herself. Haemon lunges at his father but misses and falls on his own sword in desperation. The reversal of situation is increased by one more degree when Creon's wife, on hearing the news of their son's death, commits suicide. Creon can only survey the wreckage and lament the disregard of divine law and his impetuous violence. Now he knows the truth, but it is the truth realized too late.

Characters in other dramas evince a similar passionate excess that leads to a rueful knowledge of their own errors. Philoctetes is persuaded to reverse his position and return to the Trojan war, indispensable to the Greek victory. Ajax eludes protection and takes his own life, but attains a reputation for glory nonetheless:

> You loved him.
> He was honest and just,
> he was a perfect man. (1568–70)

Deianira's suicide results from an innocent mistake: her gift to Heracles of the poisoned cloak. She dies unredeemed, mourned by her son who had accused her of treachery. Sophocles has trained his unwavering gaze on human vulnerability.

Electra attains twofold intensity by its portrayal of grief and then intrigue. The first half of the action reviews Electra's compulsive threnody. It is not so much that mourning becomes Electra as it is that Electra becomes mourning: she apologizes to the chorus for her unending refrains:

> Dear women! I am ashamed to have you think
> my laments are too many, my grief too much;
> but since I cannot help it, please forgive me. (246–48)

But hers is no state for moderate or pious conduct:

> My outrageous life has taught me how
> to do outrageous things. (213–14)

Both main elements of the play's craftily fashioned plot emerge in the opening exchange between the heroine and the chorus of Mycenean women. Electra's vengeful anger builds, shared in collusion with her sister, Chrysothemis, and sharpened in bitter invective by her confrontation of Clytemnestra with its nearing indictment of her mother's guilt. Following the false report of Orestes' death, Electra clashes with Chrysothemis over her plan to take vengeance at all costs. The sisters have converged, only to diverge—a favored dynamic in Sophoclean dialogue. Electra's grief has faded in the heat of her passionate hatred. But when Orestes first appears, disguised as a Phocian and bearing an urn allegedly holding Orestes' ashes, the mourning mounts again to an ironic level. Electra addresses the urn in her brother's hands in plangent tones with a sweeping elegiac remembrance of their days together.

The recognition scene sets the stage for Orestes' revenge, prompted and planned by his sister's stratagem. She is no longer the sorrowful victim but the epitome of vengeful hatred, glorying in the long-awaited revenge. When Clytemnestra's death cry is heard from within the palace, Electra exults on stage, shouting "Strike her again!" She wishes Aegisthus were there . . . and soon enough he appears. Orestes has hidden inside, but Electra greets the hated husband winningly and craftily maneuvers him into the shrouded presence of the body he assumes to be that of Orestes. But it is Orestes alive who reveals himself and Aegisthus' murdered consort at the final moment before dispatching Aegisthus. As the king courageously faces his fate, Electra makes her last demand:

> . . . Kill him now, and throw his body out
> for creatures who know how to bury his kind,
> far out of sight. This is the only way
> to free me from the weight of ancient crimes. (1439–42)

The architecture of Sophocles' well-proportioned structure is complete.

King Oedipus

Translated by
Jascha Kessler

Translator's Preface

> Lord, we know what we are, but know not what we
> may be.
> — Ophelia to Claudius

When the Red Carpet was still flying, I hopped on it one fine day in June 1980, and before I knew it I'd landed in Sofia. I had visited Bulgaria the year before, invited to work at Englishing some of their poets, so I had been toured around the country and briefed on some of the lore it was thought I needed as an introduction to my task. Mainly, the theme propounded was that Bulgars regard themselves as guardians of the region known anciently as Trakis, the land where Orpheus sang heart-stopping songs that could move the rocks and trees, and then his world-stopping dirge for his lost Lady, Eurydice, though what that song was we do not know. Of course, the Bulgarians are latecomers to Thracia, which also includes modern Macedon; yet they are attached to lyric poetry and an exotic-sounding tradition of choral sacred music, the culture of which is more profound than an exploitation of the name Thrace for touristic brochures.[1] Their poetry is modeled on the lyrical forms closest to song. Song emanates from the source of what music can express of the ineffable. Music, say that music symbolized by the name of Orpheus, may perhaps be the essence of what Cudworth called, "this Love which the Cosmogonia was derived from, . . . no other than the Eternal Unmade Deity."[2] At any rate, even at that time, and under the dull, thick carapace of a quarter century's Stalinist social policy of ruthless war meant to crush the peasantry—which is what Bulgaria mostly is, peasants, their nobility having been destroyed by the Turks centuries ago, their middle class scarcely large enough to tally when Russia liberated the Bulgars toward the close of the nineteenth century—one could, in traveling about, sense something strange about this Bulgaria, something "wide-eyed, inscrutable and complex," as one of their poets has it.[3]

When I telephoned from the airport I caught the Writers Union president, Lyubomir Levchev, off-balance, and learned he was due in Moscow the next day. It seemed that my arrival, though requested, turned out to be two days later than had been proposed, so I found that the many writers invited from around the globe had already been sent down to Varna on the Black Sea. Levchev is a humorous man and a poet of quality; indeed, all the officers of the Bulgarian Writers Union were poets, which struck me as quite unusual since none of the other Soviet-model writers organizations in the Warsaw Pact's grip allowed any positions of command to their good poets (who wisely may have avoided it). He suggested to the interpreters who had been assigned me on the previous visit, "Why not take him to see Auntie Vanga tomorrow?" Both gasped with shock and delighted surprise—which suggested this was a privilege seldom accorded to visitors.[4] A taxi was secured for the 300 km drive to the southwestern town of Petric, down by the Macedonian and Greek borders. By the time things were arranged, Sofia's sidewalks had been pulled in and it was too late to obtain what was required for my audience: a sugar cube to be placed under my pillow that night.[5] I'd have to do without.

Departing from Sofia at dawn, we made a pleasant though longish jaunt to Petric. The Mayor received us around 2 P.M. There followed the usual courtesy of coffee and the customary pitch lauding his city, its agriculture, its industry. Then we followed his car out to Vanga's summer residence in the country. A fair-sized low cottage, it stood alone just off a side road. There were a little orchard and a good sized kitchen garden on one side of it, kept by the peasant family who served her. Vanga being blind, they guarded her from intruders who showed up day and night, begging a moment for even one quick question. The Mayor had been informed it would be a while—it seemed she wanted to finish the line she was knitting—so we cooled our heels next to our cars parked on the quiet, tree-shaded road. Apparently, Auntie Vanga was a "property of the State," more precisely, of the Institute for Parapsychology, so of course she took no money. That was a delicate point, however, since she brought a not inconsiderable revenue to the coffers of Petric: the cash came from limiting access to her. That protection for her was necessary was manifested as we chatted in the golden light of the mid-afternoon. I saw a well-dressed woman in black flit through the garden from the copse beyond the house, and when I asked who she could be, our drivers dashed through the gated hedge and emerged a moment later, scolding the woman as they marched her off holding her firmly by her elbows. The Mayor sighed, perhaps at the unregenerate credulity of educated people in his scientific, socialist society.

When finally admitted into the garden, we were led around to the same porch the poor woman had headed toward, which was the kitchen's back door. Inside it was cool and dark. Vanga sat at the end of a plain, oilcloth-covered pine table, in her lap a panel of the blue wool sweater they'd said she was knitting, its needles rolled up in it. She was a woman in her late sixties. Her gray hair, worn with a part down the center, was confined by a net. She wore a simple gray printed frock, the sort elderly Italian women are often to be seen in. She sat erect: calm, expressionless. I was introduced as the *Amerikanska poeta*, and placed at her right hand. Tsvetelina Nikolova and Valentin Kostov, my young interpreters, seated themselves at the table's far end, facing us.

"Where is his cube of sugar?" she demanded, but when they proffered anxiously that we hadn't had a chance to get one for me to sleep on the night before, she seemed unperturbed. She asked, "Does he wear a watch?" I took mine off and placed it in the upturned palm of her right hand. She hefted it, turned it, and then pressed it between finger and thumb. It would do. Then she began to speak—of me, yet not to me. She spoke as the blind do, chin tilted up, gazing before her as though she focused on the ceiling at the end of the room. She uttered short declarative statements: "You always keep water next to your bed! Good! Never drink iced water! You eat cold bread! It is all right! Drive, drive! All right! You will be safe!" It was as though she commenced with odd feelers, trivial non sequiturs, calibrating, finding her range.

My interpreters repeated after her, somewhat interrogatively, puzzled. I was not, however, for only I knew that I kept mineral water on my night table, and that back home our custom was to buy quality day-old loaves of bread at half-price and store them in the freezer so that they were conveniently available at any time. So, since her "gnomic declarations" were palpable hits, even her description of the arrangement of our home, my studio and its location near the sea, I could answer her each time with a tranquil "Da!"

Satisfied to have "placed" me, she barked out, and this unexpected turn fixed her authority for me, "Why did you tell me he is an American poet?" To which Tsvetelina, a quick journalist with whom I had traveled around

Bulgaria for ten days the year before, and a graduate in American studies with excellent, unaccented English, protested, "But that is what he is! Poeta Americanska!"

Vanga shook her head: "Ne, ne! He is not! He's a Jew!"[6]

Both young people with me looked at me surprised. Was it so? It had never even occurred to them that I might be Jewish. I replied simply, "Da, da!"

Vanga nodded complacently, as though saying, "What I tell you is so!"

After that opening, our interview lasted less than an hour but could have been longer had I come as a needy pilgrim to petition the oracle. It produced a series of startling if gratuitous pronouncements regarding the problems of various of my relations, and foretelling occurrences that were later corroborated. Nothing she had to say to me went beyond my personal sphere, yet everything was composed of intimate, personal details no one would have troubled to concern himself with, let alone sought to have learned about. When she understood that I wasn't anxious to hear the sort of things people go to clairvoyants hoping to be told, that indeed I had no questions to ask, she stopped and asked why she had been advised I was a poet. "Ne, ne!" she declared, I was no such person—but a philosopher! Naturally my young companions were baffled. I too was puzzled, but not really surprised.[7] There is a profound level at which the two discourses, psychologically speaking at least, sometimes overlap and meld.

She then proceeded to demonstrate her power, and indeed power was what she possessed and wielded. Peremptorily, she demanded to know why I hadn't brought my wife to meet her. When I replied that I had flown here from California, many thousands of kilometers to the west, she asked if we had never at home consulted a "prophet." I told her candidly that in fact there was a dear friend, a woman like herself, but she too lived far from us (in Oregon, as it happened). Vanga said earnestly that we must go and talk to this woman, adding matter-of-factly, "It is what we are here for![8] Understand this!" I reassured her that I did talk to our friend during the year, and in the past had consulted her about myself and others in hours of difficulty. She nodded approval.

"But," I queried her in turn, "why do you want to know?" To which she gave this reason: there was someone who had just made herself known, and it was urgent.

"Who do you know in Hungary!" I had been to Budapest many times; I have many friends in Budapest. "Ne, ne! She is dead!" My wife comes of Hungarian-born parents, I offered. Vanga acknowledged this, and, yes, now she recognized who it was—my wife's mother (who died in 1973).[9] When, to test her, I asked about my father-in-law (who died in 1953), she waved her hand, dismissing it, "Oh, he's too far away now." Whoever she was "seeing" was terribly worried about her daughter. ("Worried" was a favorite expression of my mother-in-law, who was herself given to anticipating imminent misfortune.) When I asked what troubled her, Vanga said, "Your wife's sister is all blackness where her lungs should be, black like an x-ray picture" (not that she, who it was said had gone blind at thirteen, might ever have seen an x-ray plate). That was most interesting. I understood what she was saying: the woman in danger had already undergone eleven lung operations over two torturous decades, suffering repeated surgery to remove recurring nodes of a rare kind of malignancy, a muscle-tissue type that had escaped from the uterus. (Five years after Vanga "saw" her condition, it killed her.)

Vanga nodded, and went on to discuss other matters. She described the persons and professions of other members of my wife's family, their misfortunes and afflictions. An interesting example may be offered. After having observed that politics was surely not my metier, she saw this woman's husband addressing an international audience of thousands in New York, "like the United Nations."[10] She mentioned the future of my children. I shall not go into other odd comments she made about me, but only note that when she was finished with her deliverances she requested with some urgency that, on my return to Sofia, I must insist to Georgi Djagarov that he was to come here to Petric to talk to her.[11] She took it as a given that I would meet him again during my visit to Bulgaria.

We found ourselves in Sofia that evening in the restaurant below the Writers Union, where various poets kept shyly approaching our table to ask what Vanga was like, how it gone for me with her—it seemed the buzz had flown about town all that day. I was scarcely surprised when Georgi Djagarov arrived toward 10:30, sat down to eat with us, and inquired about my visit to Petric. When at the close of my sketch of Auntie Vanga I added that she'd insisted I must persuade him to go to her, Djagarov smiled and shrugged apologetically: much as he might wish for an hour with the fortune-teller—for the sake, say, of satisfying an intellectual curiosity?—it was of course out of the question that a man in his position should visit the clairvoyant. When I suggested that perhaps it might have something to do with Israel and the United Nations, a topic on which she had begun to dilate,[12] Djagarov smiled, shrugged, and said, "All the more so, Jascha—now you can see why I can't go? But what did you think of Vanga?"

I opined that she was indeed a phenomenon.

Never mind what people believe possible or impossible, scientifically true or untrue, credible or incredible; never mind whether Vanga was a telepath (and what is that!) who "read" the contents of my mind and interpreted x-ray pictures I myself had never seen of my sister-in-law's lungs—a formidable trick, if that was her gift. What struck me about the way she gazed with blind eyes into the shadows at the end of that kitchen was the suggestion that a vast field of time seemed to lie spread before her, sub specie æternitatis, as it were spatially; that in her contemplation and recital there was neither past, nor present, nor future, but simply one immediate background against which she had seen me and mine, those who were ill or dying, and also the dead.[13] Djagarov took it in thoughtfully, and said nothing. The number 2 man in a dialectical materialist state could say nothing, of course. A casual "Da, da!" could suffice to take him down.

We can leave it at that.[14]

The priests of Apollo at Delphi served a woman, the Pythia. The site itself was holy from remotest times, from pre-Greek antiquity. The legend of Apollo's rule has it that a chthonian monster had been killed there. The place was venerated as the center of the earth, marked by the famous omphalos, although what is to be seen there today as the navel-stone is not an original artifact but a Byzantine capital. There probably was no such thing during most of Delphi's importance; hence one must suppose that the omphalos is metaphorical and signifies "the source," woman. Originally, a source is "virgin." From the virgin whose virginity is "sacrificed" there comes another virgin. In the poetry of myth that issues in doctrine she is perforce a virgin, in real life perhaps a virgin actually sacrificed, as in fertility cults that have been observed into our time in Africa. In any case there is implied the navel-cord, which ties us to the mother, and, as Joyce's Stephen Dedalus wittily put it: "by successive anastomosis of navelcords."[15]

It is not negligible that Dionysus took over and ruled in Delphi for three months during the winter of the year, during which period Apollo retreated far to the north, nor that the Dionysiac festivals at the shrine were orgiastic, women officially being sent from all the cities of Greece to partake in those rites. Neither is it negligible that the Pythia spoke from a state of frenzy, seated on her tripod, divining in an ecstasy that relates her to the most ancient, sacrificial traditions invoking the earth-spirit at that holy place. Finally, it is not negligible that Boeotia, the land of Thebes, an agricultural region famous for its horses, was the region of such important ancient cults, including the shrine of the Muses on Helicon, the cults of Eros and of Apollo himself, as well as an archaic worship of Aphrodite, among others. The Pythia's deliverances, commonly given in verse, were for a thousand years and more the most important and respected oracles in the Greek world, as compared with those rational, "sane" divinations to be construed from the reading of a liver, from the flight of birds, or from the constellations, alluded to and derided in Sophocles' play of Oedipus, where the protagonist's story is knotted inextricably to ancient Delphi's preternatural prophecies.

As we all know, the plot of *King Oedipus* unravels a mystery, to use a metaphor that may remind us of the thread unwound by Theseus as he marched into the penetralia of the Cretan labyrinth in search the Minotaur's nasty doss.[16] The mystery of Oedipus is fundamental: it is the mystery of origins. How things have come to be is in every sense the first of all questions. It is at once the cosmogonic alpha and omega, as well as our own painful mundane question, and it remains unanswered. For Oedipus, it is revealed as the fatal question whose solution the hero pursues after having learned casually he is not the child of the royal parents who raised him from infancy. In the twentieth century, this question has reverberated ever since Freud seized on its formula and applied it as a heuristic matrix, so to speak, for the investigation and understanding of problems of childhood and adolescent growth, and made his brilliant concept one of the most powerful formulations ever developed for the study of human psychology.[17] The riddle of the Sphinx is not resolved in the action of Sophocles' drama, if only because the hero had already construed it long before. When it is described elsewhere, the terrible quiz seems little more than a conundrum for a child; nevertheless it proved psychoanalytically indispensable to one of Freud's brilliant disciples, the anthropologist Geza Róheim, who discussed its symbolism in terms of the "primal scene" motif.[18]

The plethora of fascinating studies of myth and folklore that have been made since the beginnings of Romanticism in the latter eighteenth century have offered varied and indeed wonderful perspectives for our view of the non-rational and irrational components of humanity's history and societies, helping us in the west to keep in mind that motto carved in stone in the temple at Delphi: *Know thyself*.[19] On which quest, the retracing of our historical and psychological origins, our phylo- and ontogenetic legacies, as it were, has been the essential task of the modern epoch, including, first, the deciphering of the planet's geological vicissitudes and their few fossil remains, and then Darwin's study of living things and their evolution from earlier forms, an investigation that will be completed only when and if the first living thing can be known. All these vast concerns have in our era been the background against which our own appreciation of the stuff Sophocles had available to him for his drama has had to be rearranged. Oedipus' bold and stubborn insistence on discovering the source of the Theban plague, the actions he takes that lead to the climax in absolute horror at his unwitting incest, whether heroic, as is his character, or foolish, as Jocasta tries to suggest,[20] can still thrill an audience.[21]

The ancient expiation of crime and guilt afforded by sacrifice and prayer in holy places and its vicarious expiation in the catharsis of tragic (Greek) drama remain today not only a strong force but also a useful and good viaticum to those who are willing to suspend their disbelief and give imagination its due. An audience knows the story that will be told, yet it must suffer its telling in a performance by actors who simulate fictive persons (who are thereby rendered fictive even if they were historically real persons). And yet, all concessions made, one may still wonder whether the crime committed and the punishment meted out in *King Oedipus* makes sense on its face, catharsis or no, and whether the mystery is completely disclosed by its end or even afterward, or whether it can ever be disclosed in human time. I do not refer to the issue of justice, or to the cruelty of the gods, to Zeus and his Iron Law. All this has been hashed over forever, and that includes the great issues of Fate or Doom pondered not only in Athens but in Jerusalem. On reflection, one is not quite satisfied by even a thoroughly undergone catharsis and enlightenment in this work of theater. There remains something in the drama and beyond it, something in it yet not of it.

I think the clue is to be found in the final speech of the play, whose words also must be set against what we have heard earlier during Oedipus' struggle with Tiresias. In the ultimate chorus, the Theban Elder tells us that nothing can be said about the greatness or success of a life until that life is over, rounded by the big sleep, to travesty Prospero's phrase. The story must be played out until there is nothing more. Yet this piece of sententious wisdom is not uttered until we have accompanied Oedipus toward that familiar, foregone conclusion. It is the last thing we hear.

Classical tragedy shows us the agony of the fall from happiness, which is the inborn animal goal and hope of each of us, and we suffer in the vicarious experience of that loss. Surely it was suffered all the more bitterly by the audience who attended Sophocles' theater in his time, since there was no strong conception of a paradisal existence hereafter or anywhere else in the Classical world, unless you will suppose hope subsists in the form of shadows fleeting past the visitor's eye in some netherworld, as Homer shows them, or rattling by with the sound of dead leaves rushed along the ground by death's chill wind.[22] Joyce's young peripatetic, Dedalus, discourses on tragedy to his salacious-minded interlocutor, Lynch, toward the end of *A Portrait of the Artist as a Young Man*, emending Aristotle on drama, as he claims. Dedalus says: "Pity is the feeling which arrests the mind in the presence of whatsoever is grave and constant in human sufferings and unites it with the human sufferer. Terror is the feeling which arrests the mind in the presence of whatsoever is grave and constant in human sufferings and unites it with the secret cause."[23] If we feel pity for Oedipus, if we feel united with him in empathy, we do so despite our recognition that his sufferings are extraordinary beyond the usual heroic extraordinary; indeed, they are sui generis. Moreover we must also must agree that his situation is certainly not a constant for most of humanity, although (*pace* Freud) it may well universally be a potential, latent psychic reality, let us even admit, a "virtual" reality, since Jocasta herself forthrightly suggests it as such. Nevertheless, the facts of his case are neither grave nor constant human occurrences. We feel terror, nevertheless, perhaps because we are bonded in sympathy with the secret cause of his sufferings. If so, we must look farther for that secret cause. And to do that we must consider the phenomenon of Tiresias.

There are persons who seem to have certain gifts, if you will, or powers, as I prefer to think of them, of sight or insight unavailable to almost everyone else. Call those powers uncanny. It is unnecessary and in fact useless to argue about such things from a rational or empirical, philosophical, or scientific perspective, where replication of the test is correctly considered the only touchstone that can be respected.[24] The very question of such a thing as foretelling is begged by the phenomenon of "prophecy," which by its very nature offers each of its instances as a singleton. Since the arguments concerning augury are already announced, considered, and dismissed in Sophocles' play of Oedipus, most powerfully by Jocasta, we can pass over the tangled and messy history of clairvoyance in the age of positivism that commenced with Mesmer in the mid-eighteenth century and devolved into many and various pseudomystical, obscurantist offshoots both secular and religious, as in the charismatic cults of our time, not to mention run-of-the-mill, popular "psychics" who are simply silly predictors whose record of "hits" is as good as nil.

It is a trivial rejoinder to contend that Tiresias' prediction of the king's end—that he will himself be led forth blind from Thebes before the matter for which the seer had been summoned there is concluded—is itself foreknown to the writer of the play and must therefore be subsumed, both within the drama and in our criticism of it, as purely or merely ironic. Of course it is that, too. Of more interest today, perhaps, when this most famous of tragedies has been so familiar in all its aspects for so many centuries, is the matter of prophecy, which beyond the commonplace *frissons* provided by ineradicable superstition[25] may open up into a philosophical vista, even the perspectives of contemporary physics and its still untested, perhaps even untestable theory.[26] It is not a question of *proving* any sort of knowledge regarding what has not yet come or is already past.

Shakespeare is properly modern on this head. Feste sings in *Twelfth Night*, "What's to come is still unsure."[27] In *Macbeth*, however, there is genuine prophecy, albeit so equivocal its significance is contingent on action, or free will. Those to whom the Three Weird Women (Norns? Fates? perhaps even Muses?) speak are not constrained to realize their destiny. Unlike Oedipus, Macbeth is given, as it were, alternatives: to do or not to do.[28] Macduff, a beneficiary of the despot's evil, is made aware of his future as a result of those deeds. It is Hamlet who expresses the view implicit in the tragedy of the post-Classical world, a view that contains willed action on the part of the agonist: "There's a divinity that shapes our ends, Roughhew them how we will." Again, that is not what we see in this play, which commences with an inquiry into the cause of the ghastly devastation of Thebes, an evil emanating from the natural world, not an assault brought against its walls by human agents. There is evil, yet all are innocent; there is a crime, yet it is not the fault of any one's having willed a crime. We learn that a rational question has been put to the god; concomitantly there is a desperate if skeptical resort to the one person who may explain the god's answer, an old man named Tiresias.[29]

So far as is known, Sophocles had available to him two legends regarding Tiresias, a blind seer of archaic Thebes who was so highly regarded that even his ghost as Homer describes him in the *Odyssey* is the single living spirit in Hades, and no mere phantasmal figure. He was, in one tradition, both wise and blind because he had seen Athena bathing; she spared his life but blinded him, offering as recompense the power of prophecy, yet only because his mother was her friend. In another tradition, he came across two serpents coupling and struck them with his staff,[30] whereupon he was transmogrified into a woman. Later in his life the same thing occurred: Tiresias struck at the coupling snakes and was turned into a man again. When Hera and Zeus were in dispute as to which sex had the greater pleasure in making love, the only one they could turn to was Tiresias, who had experienced it in both bodies. When Tiresias declared that it was the woman who enjoyed the act more, an angry Hera blinded him, no doubt for his truthful candor; but to make up for the injury, Zeus awarded him long life and the power to foretell future events. Such a history and reputation carries an aura of the metaphysical; on the other hand, it was said of Tiresias that he died as a very old man during the evacuation of Thebes when it was besieged by the Seven: he stopped to quench his thirst at the spring Tilphussa, and its exceedingly cold water was too much for him. In any case, the legends are long behind him when he is called to Thebes by Oedipus, where he appears as what he is: a dignified, respected, blind ancient led by a boy.

We learn from Oedipus in the very first scene that he has been sent for to advise the King, concomitantly with Creon's mission to Delphi to seek the oracle's advice. As it happens, although it is never mentioned by Sophocles, Apollo had once warned Laius of the death that would come to him from the son he was to have because Laius had earlier abducted Chrysippus the son of Pelops, who had given him shelter during his exile from Thebes. It seems to have been a consequence of the law of talion.[31] It is interesting that Pelops himself was married to a woman whose husband he had killed, and that that king was her father as well as her husband, a kind of mirror reversal of the situation in Thebes a generation later.[32] All this matter was known to

Tiresias, of course, and since what was foredoomed has come to pass, he refuses to divulge any of it to Oedipus. How can he? Why should he? What good can it do? And that is what he says on entering the scene.

Our contemporary curiosity is a form of idle prurience; perhaps it is morbidly infantile, though it is anything but innocent. It may be that that which seeks only to know is an obscene, empty desperation.[33] And it is here that the difficult moral situation of the seer as a phenomenon is to be found. If the gods alone know, those immortals who seem to see the entire pattern of time from their vantage which is both in and yet out of time, and if they are themselves powerless to change things—unwilling to try to use their will to change things, as it seems to Homeric Greece—the position of the mortal who also sees is one that requires not only the virtue of patience, but a tactful silence in the presence of the inevitable, which to such a person somehow pre-exists. There is no logic here that is not intrinsically circular. And there is no quantum statistical number available to be ascribed as an equivalent to sheer chance, luck, dark ignorance, or whatever. Not to Tiresias, not to the Pythia, a Sibyl, not to Vanga. Reluctant to satisfy Oedipus, whom he has foreknown to be what he is, to become who he has become, Tiresias will not reveal his full knowledge until forced. Threatened with violence, he finally tells Oedipus before the citizens of the city that by the time the day is out we will see him tottering blindly from Thebes, leaning on a stick. It is a terrible thing to have to say and impossible for Oedipus to have to hear, even as we watch it happen. For indeed we dread the knowledge that we do not, cannot ever know what the next hour brings.

Tiresias does know. He always did. Yet it seems that people such as he regard it as pointless to tell us what they see, if they see, since such knowledge is useless. This was the old Greek fatalist submission to Zeus' Iron Law. We think differently. We imagine it is in the paradoxical nature of what is not yet that yet it is, and is to come. We live, as Bergson describes it, on the moving crest of the wave of the present into the future, if we think of time's direction as a moving forward; or else we wait in the instantaneous yet unmoving moment until the moving wave of the future passes over or through us in our present, so that we are conscious of a succession of such moments. The metaphysics, rather the physics, of time remains an open secret: it would seem, at least to some of us, that our consciousness knows, yet does not know what or how it knows. Bergson, our contemporary, considered chance, progress, and evolution as part of the creative movement forward that creates time itself. In any case, we do not know Time itself. For Tiresias there is no such thing. He is in Hades, as Homer says, dead yet deathless.

What all this amounts to in terms of an aesthetic of tragedy such as is supplied by Joyce's definition is that the terror aroused in the mind by our perception of "the secret cause of human suffering" is here demonstrated by Sophocles, who lived ninety years; it comes from the fact that the future not only is but is already known, although not to you and me. The stories the tragic poets tell us are familiar stories, and perhaps the catharsis Aristotle discusses is effected through our presence at their enactment, more precisely, their reenactment in the ritual of the theater, a way for us to be taught to reconcile ourselves to an arresting fact in human existence. It is not that we must die, which is hard enough to accept, even if it is believed to be the case (and not by any means do we all believe that we die completely and forever, and fewer still among us can for that matter easily accept it), but that we perforce live blindly, unable to see the very next step to be taken in time. This is terrible to a conscious mind. That we do take the next step is perhaps possible only because ingrained in us is what the philosopher Santayana calls our "animal faith." The protagonists of tragic drama, however, are made to take those steps: we watch in rising anxiety and fear, and we undergo with them their sufferings—at a safe distance from their imagined reality—in order to learn or come to comprehend that those steps must be taken, even though a terrible future already exists, and abides their coming.

In our own world, however, it seems there are some beings who do see all before it comes to pass, and not only the future.[34] Tiresias represents this type. In their presence one feels awe, for one must acknowledge that the sighted are blind to time future. Whether literally blind or not, these people see what we cannot, and they sometimes say what ought not to be uttered. They see that it is there; they see that it will be here; and of course they see it as it presents itself to the present hour.

It is unsurprising that so little has been made in drama and legend of a person such as Tiresias, since his sort (when it is not a public figure like that of the Pythia at Delphi) is beyond the reach of our comprehension. Sometimes someone like that appears in one's life at a crucial juncture.[35] In *King Oedipus* Tiresias is a principal personage who is usually thought of as merely instrumental to impelling the plot into motion, the first of the play's several fateful messengers, when in fact he is someone beyond the extraordinary, while paradoxically within the realm of mundane possibility.

And then there is his chthonic, legendary connection to the other unknowns—the women, whether mortal or divine or emanations of the natural world. The women, here represented by Jocasta, were present long before and during Classical times; they remain mostly unknown to history, even today, even to themselves, perhaps unknown to all men but a Tiresias, who had shared their remarkable powers. We have the name of another such woman, mentioned vaguely and by a hint. She is Diotima, Socrates' advisor in love, if that is the term, a legendary, sibylline figure, a priestess of Mantinea, a mountainous region of villages that had preserved many archaic myths and cults. Yet even there our information is second-hand, since it is not Socrates himself who tells us of her but Plato, who in the *Symposium* writes that his teacher had learned about the metaphysic of Eros from her. In any case, we ought in experiencing the agony of Oedipus to wonder at it that there is one principal who acts yet remains untouched by it all, Tiresias. If we try to watch the denouement of the king's tragedy as though from *his* vantage, it must fill the mind and heart with a true and limitless dread. Surely it places us in the Greek: all is always foredoomed; to see all through the eyes of Tiresias as fully foreknown is unbearable.

Finally, it also may be useful to imagine ourselves looking at the "matter of Oedipus" through the tragic poet's eyes in his own time, while thinking about what he dealt with, but from our situation. We are all our mothers' sons—and daughters, too. What more, apart from a pious duty to inter her vanquished dead brother, was Antigone defending when she resisted Creon in later years, if not the respect owed her mother's child? Is the ancestry of Jocasta known, after all? It is not even stated.[36] In Oedipus' kingship itself there is tripartite rule: his queen and her brother Creon share the power, as Creon himself reminds him.[37] Interpreters, transfixed by the abomination of the incest that has produced Antigone, her sister, and their two brothers, will not have pondered sufficiently on the story, whose structure lies within the trilogy's engrossing drama, a "history" that may itself be taken as an instructive if very large mythical metaphor. I mean, taken as the poetry that formulates a transition from the most ancient and chthonic forms of fertility religion, in which females support its foundation—as objects of worship, as embodiments of the cult, as its administrators, served sometimes by priests—females who in fact remain to this hour the sine qua non of our species. It is a transition to the cultural superstructures of male lordship wielding the instruments and powers of *tekné*, both literally and intellectually. Zeus became the paramount god of the Hellenic Pantheon. In Jerusalem there was eventually but the one Lord: no female or other gods are visible in Judaism.[38] In the Classical world, the millennial cults of the women lingered on until at last the power at Delphi was but a remnant of a vestige.

The strange figure of Tiresias, who seems to have "neither youth nor age," as Eliot, referring to some unnamed male, put it abstractly in *Gerontion*, stands in Thebes as the last human recourse against the country's obliteration. He is also the last resource of the saving knowledge that comes of knowing, or having known, the archaic women, like his own mother, who was a "friend of Athena." It is to him as well as to Delphi that Oedipus must turn in order to know what was and what will be. The drama pivots on Tiresias, who when forced to speak points to Delphi too, that is, to the Pythia, the priestess through whom Apollo is said to speak. For Tiresias knows. Indeed, he always knew that it is woman who holds not only the ancient power but the only true power. And it is woman, gradually demoted and defiled, who wreaks ultimate revenge. Her secret, as the myth states it, is that she has the greater pleasure in love (and procreation), and it is Tiresias himself who tells Zeus so, as noted earlier, for which he's punished by Hera—for revealing the secret of the woman.[39] There is a context to the contest, and it is transcendently archaic. And yet it should come as no great revelation to anyone who considers that mythical story, or its poetry, if you will. When Tiresias departs, what follows in the dramas of Oedipus, as the legends tell us, is nothing but struggle and warfare, until the Epigoni who represent the party of Jocasta, in short her lineage, are in the end defeated.

From this distance in time, it may be imagined that the tragedy, as Sophocles seems to have understood and presented it, transcends Oedipus and Thebes. Sophocles is himself looking back at what "happened" long ago, before Homer sang.[40] His Periclean Athens is already a new world, though named for the daughter of Zeus and for Zeus. It is already given over, and indeed was irretrievably given over long before, to what was to supplant myth and poetry—philosophy—and to all that through the centuries to come was to turn into our world, known until recently as Western Civilization, itself now receding from us. Indeed it, too, has already slipped as far into the past as the legends of ancient Thebes, which were old when in the *Odyssey* Homer mentions in passing the misfortune of Jocasta (called Epicaste).

After Oedipus has atoned for what was inflicted on him, and to which he bore witness bravely, heroically, and after he was buried, that ancient power from the line of the mother continued to be evoked as the power to foresee, to heal, and to reconcile. Oedipus was caused to suffer for the sin of his father and for the crimes of those who followed after. It is not an altogether unfamiliar form of "Mystery." The trilogy may be taken to signify both an end and a beginning. As for what was begun then, we have not yet seen it all.[41]

Notes

1. As the scholar/poet Aleksandar Shurbanov put it, "The soil on which the Bulgarian state first came into being in the seventh century was redolent with the words and melodies of songs so enchanting that the wild animals of the forest, even the very trees, could be made to come and listen to them in awe. For this was the land of the Thracian bard Orpheus, whom the ancient world revered as a demigod and whose descendants had been merged with the invading Slavic and Turkic tribes into a complex that was to become known as the Bulgarian people. Although the songs of Orpheus have not survived, the Bulgarians have always been conscious of his legacy of magic, and in much of present-day Bulgarian poetry the chthonic Orphic rapport with nature, and with the native land, may be discerned." One might add to this that Orpheus himself seems to have been a latecomer to this place, and that its legends and religion are lost in a darkness that is older than archaic Greece itself. Pindar and Plato seem to have had insight into what was later called Orphism, a system of mystical beliefs and disciplines, the teachings of which were attributed to Orpheus. The place, in short, is old as old can be, in Indo-European terms, at least.

2. Ralph Cudworth, *The True Intellectual System of the Universe*, i. iv. § 14. 250 (1678). The Neo-Platonism of Cudworth, epitomized here, is somewhat reminiscent of Orphic doctrine. Looking ahead to my later observations, it can be suggested that the lamentations of Orpheus for his wife may be recognized as a farewell to some lost "order of things." Eurydice was pursued, it will be remembered, by a son of Apollo, Aristaeus. She was bitten by a snake as she fled, and taken away to the underworld. Orpheus might yet have preserved her, and the world of her sisters (and her nymphs), had he not looked back. What is the meaning of that prohibition, which has not been properly explained, that is, read as a figure of speech? After all, even his wife's name signifies something to do with power, "she who judges over all," or simply "princess." There came a point under the Apollonian establishment where the one who sang for Eurydice was forbidden to do so: and indeed, by persisting in his song of lamentation after she had been lost forever—which stopped the course of Nature—Orpheus too was dismembered, to speak literally as well as figuratively, although his head went singing on, floating from Thrace to wash up, where? Where else? On the island of Lesbos! Metaphorically, the ancient cult itself had been broken up, or dismembered.

3. Luchezar Elenkov, "Concerned with Something Else While Turnovo's Dying," trans. Jascha Kessler with Aleksandar Shurbanov, *Nimrod* (awards volume) 26, 1 (1968): 37.

4. I can think of only one other, John Cheever, and it is simply a surmise based on his last novel, *Oh, What a Paradise It Seems* (1982). Its protagonist is taken to meet a Sybil in her "cave" in Bulgaria, and what he learns changes his life. Cheever, whose later life saw a dramatic change indeed, had been toured through Bulgaria by the State Department some few years earlier, as had John Updike. I wonder whether Updike visited Vanga as well, although I have not seen it in his work.

5. I did not at that time associate the piece of sugar with the ancient Greek "medical" cure known as "incubation" practiced at the great Aesculapian spa of Epidaurus, but supposed merely that something that had been in contact with my person was a sort of surrogate, not unfamiliar to some diviners' techniques today. It is, however, a kind of "crystal."

6. In fact, she spoke but one word, "Zhid!" I knew that word and its use. In Bulgaria it is not a proper word; only a peasant speaking in the old way could or would use it, since it is scarcely denotative, but a forceful slur, equivalent to our "kike."

7. It struck me even at that instant that she was alluding, uncannily, to a poem I'd written over a quarter century earlier and later published in my first collection, *Whatever Love Declares* (Los Angeles: Plantin Press, 1969), "Philosophical Transactions at Montauk." The middle stanza suggests a philosophical naturalism. Vanga apparently descried that structure of my "belief," for later on she reverted to the subject of faith, asking me what my religion was, as if she had quite forgotten, having denominated me at the outset as a Jew. She meant by it something else at that point, however; something to do with "God," spoken in terms of herself as interpreter of one's disposition in life.

> Even God deserts his echoes: silence
> confounds the drone of antique deliberations
> whose heavens were harsher than life: dismissed,
> our elders trudged to their tabernacles
> in the moral fires, leaving us this world.
> Is it strange to be content to be hopeless?
> Consider burrowing nations of clams,
> or fat porgies scrounging those taut fish lines.
> If marrow's not nectar, must it be bilge?
> We put our questions: answers never come.

8. Later she told Tsvetelina that the one who would replace her after she was gone had already been born elsewhere in Bulgaria. Vanga knew who the girl was, though her parents did not. The implication of her casual understanding is that there had always been a chain of such seers in unbroken succession. As she put it, "It's what we are here for!"

9. Of course I also marveled that a monolingual old Bulgarian peasant woman, as she termed herself in a little while when she started to comment about the current state of affairs in Israel (the invasion of Lebanon and siege of Beirut were underway at that hour), recognized a revenant as a Hungarian-speaker—and, moreover, understood him.

10. Which also proved accurate: about six months later he was elected President of the International Association of Political Scientists and gave his inaugural talk where she had said he would—in New York. I was not to hear about that event until it was quite some time in the past for him!

11. Djagarov, a poet (who lobbied for the Nobel Prize later on in vain), was Deputy Head of

State, number 2 man under the Premier, and the very first person I had been taken to meet on my arrival in Sofia the year before. He sought me out at the Writers Union cafe at a "private" audience in a lounge walled by glass but closed to the main part of the place, where all the many writers that afternoon were forced to sit and cool their heels crowded together for a good long hour in the small anteroom where they took their coffee and drinks. Newcomers approaching the locked glass stood surprised, staring in at us, their expressions saying, "Djagarov! Here? Who is that with him?" while I was checked out, rather "grilled" by him . . . on poetry, politics, and general questions concerning life in the United States. And the word is "grilled," in the sense of brusque interrogation. We became good friends immediately, and remained so until his death some years later.

12. "Now, as for Israel, this is what is going to happen—but, I shouldn't talk about it, I'm only an ignorant peasant woman . . ."

13. I was to hear 10 months afterward that she had promised a skeptical Tsvetelina (bitterly divorced from her very early marriage) that she should be married in 6 months, a prediction scoffed at by that proud young woman, who declared that there were no eligible men in Sofia she had not already rejected. I was in fact acquainted with her future groom, who served as an interpreter for the French guests of the Writers Union; and indeed I was to give him a lift to the airport in my cab two weeks later when I left Sofia, though the two were strangers to one another on the day of Vanga's forecast. But that is another anecdote.

14. Vanga died in 1996, after causing a shrine for herself to be built outside Petric. Was it vanity, or was it with the intention to mark a place where, as Eliot put it in *Little Gidding* (1942) "prayer has been valid"? The poet goes on to say, "the communication / Of the dead is tongued with fire beyond the language of the living." To be sure, Vanga when alive spoke herself in words that were tongued in homely speech. It was for those who lived to verify for themselves later whatever truth she spoke.

15. In *Ulysses*. Coincidentally, apart from the "master artificer" after whom Joyce named his hero, there was also ancient Boeotia's "Daedala," a sacred marriage, apparently accompanied by a fire-ceremony. "Daedal" itself originates in the chthonic, the arising from earth, in fertility rites, hence in connection with marriage and procreation.

16. Interestingly, one version of Theseus' adventures shows him being helped on his way by an old woman (Hecale), whom he finds dead on his return from the slaying of the Minotaur, the man-bull monstrously born to Pasiphae, whose unnatural lust was inflicted on her by the gods. She herself seems to have been simply queen and wife to Minos. Theseus, an emulator of Heracles, is the Athenian hero, for he it was who relieved Athens and Attica of the onerous tribute of seven maidens and seven youths sent each year to the Bull of Crete. In Crete the wall paintings at Knossos show us youthful acrobats dancing on the backs of bulls, not attacking them. The legends may reflect historical conflicts between a youthful Athens and ancient cultures. Whether these annual fourteen offerings were sacrificed in Crete or not, the metaphor tells us about something that remains to this day in its attenuated form a living part of Mediterranean culture in the form of the bull rings of Spain and Mexico. In the Camargue, I think, the bull is not killed but "danced" with.

17. That it troubled him in so many ways is evident from his insistence at the very end of his life on the publication of the unsettling monograph, *Moses and Monotheism*, in which the tale of the origin of this hero is analyzed and the answer found to be the very inverse of what we are told in the Bible. Like Oedipus, discovered by a shepherd, Moses, too, was no slave's abandoned foundling, but instead the son of the Pharaoh's daughter.

18. Cf. Róheim, *The Riddle of the Sphinx* (1934) and *Animism, Magic, and the Divine King* (1930). Other considerations have been brought forward since Freud and Róheim mulled

the matter. What has usually been overlooked is the fact that the Sphinx, a dreadful kind of oracle in and of herself, asks the question, whereas the oracle's role is to answer questions. This inversion of function seems rather striking. That the Sphinx kills those who reply wrongly is contrary to the rule of providing sanctuary and solace to the seeker of truth. The winged Sphinx who held Seven-Gated Thebes in her thrall leaped from her perch on the mountainside to her death on hearing Oedipus' solution, so that one wonders what her wings were for. Perhaps the reply should have been different, since an oracle's questions and answers refer not to generalities but to the petitioner or seeker or, indeed, sacrificial victim who approaches it. In this case, it is not only Everyman who crawls in infancy, walks upright in maturity, and limps away leaning on a stick in hebetude, but also Oedipus, whose feet were crippled in infancy, who walked as a hero, and leaves Thebes blinded, feeling his way with his staff, as the seer predicts. Hence the truer answer to her riddle will have been, "It is Oedipus himself!" If we read the metaphor, the Sphinx is itself a representation of ourselves, who have been born to exist in a bestial body, who wear a human (i.e., intelligent) head, and who may come to wear the wings of the divine spirit that sometimes seems latent or potential in us. This suggestion concludes a fascinating study of the legend's origins in historical reality, not myth. Cf. Immanuel Velikovsky, *Oedipus and Akhnaton* (1960).

19. This motto is itself an ambiguous sort of oracle. It challenges us to discover an identity that is always different from itself, as Heraclitus pointed out nearly a century before Sophocles wrote his play. It would seem that Oedipus does indeed know who he is, and proclaims it proudly in this play. He does not, however, know what he is, for that knowledge is given only to Tiresias. (Sophocles' audience presumably was aware of his progenitor's proclivity as a pederast.)

20. "So many men have slept with their mothers, / and made love to them as well—in their dreams!" (1091–92).

21. Even if the taboo is often broken, and broken agreeably, too, or so we are meant to think, even "harmlessly," and successfully, as for example in a film like Louis Malle's *Murmur of the Heart* (1971), in which the son is still a pubescent boy. F. Scott Fitzgerald did not think it was so easy, for it drove his heroine Nicole Diver mad'in *Tender Is the Night*, his most ambitious novel, and may have been the source of his wife Zelda's ultimate collapse and confinement. Perhaps the present uproar over the ubiquity of father/daughter incest, which seems not to be as much condemned when it is mother/son incest, suggests something about our species' status that Freud brought very much into contention, one that is far from understood in modern primate studies. The novelist Michael Blankfort proposed quite seriously in his last work that a psychoanalyst could take his grown daughter, a divorcée, as his mistress, and that the long relationship would help them both to maturity and stability; that is, eating and having one's cake is permissible and possible. Sons appear to be much more intimidated by the Mother (the Medusa?) than daughters by fathers, to whom their helplessness as female children and their desire as females makes them pathetically subject. That may reflect the differences between the physiology as well as the developmental psychology of the male and female. On the other hand, the ancient Mitanni, whose language was so far as is known neither Aryan nor Semitic, and who were renowned for horse-breeding (which might argue an Asiatic, e.g., Scythian origin), were it seems ritually fixed to mother/son marriage; their rule extended to the east of the Hurrian, later Assyrian empires. The recognized power of Phoenician women is remarked in the story of King Ahab. It may have been the case in Canaanite culture, too, that female dominance was long in being diminished. There are, in short, reasons for expecting some kind of eventual ground-

ing for some of the legends that arose in the West, long before Periclean Athens. (See Veli-kovsky on the question of Akhnaton.)

22. An image to be found in the Sumerian epic of Gilgamesh, gorgeously if paradoxically used by Milton millennia later describing the fallen host of rebel angels in Paradise Lost. When Shelley saw those same dried leaves swept along in a vision of the year's death and hoped for some return in the Spring, perhaps he was combining the ancient trope with a natural-istic notion of a resurrection, on the order of the physicist today who tells us that our life is based on the carbon that comes from supernovas and that our elements will eventually be "recycled" into and out of the alembic of a Black Hole.

23. In the same discourse, Dedalus explains the paucity of, indeed lack of possibility for, true tragedy in the modern world, largely because of a cultural confusion arising from the decline of tragedy into pathos, and pathos and sentimentality into didactic, "kinetic" pornography. The world we have lived in since the rise of the middle class, perhaps since Christianity itself, has made tragedy in the Classic mode unlikely. Arthur Miller argued in the 1950s that a tragic play could only be written about the family. That, too, has grown improbable with the decline of the family structure, in totalist and capitalist societies alike.

24. Freud touched on it with rational analysis in a short essay, "The Uncanny," which, though it answers its questions, mainly about cases of déjà vu, does not ask the questions put to us by the case of Tiresias, nor by Auntie Vanga for that matter, not to mention my experience of the realm of the unknowable over 35 years through the "vision" of my own late friend.

25.

> To communicate with Mars, converse with spirits,
>
> . . . . .
>
> To explore the womb, or tomb, or dreams; all these are usual
> Pastimes and drugs, and features of the press:
> And always will be, some of them especially
> When there is distress of nations and perplexity
> Whether on the shores of Asia, or in the Edgware Road.
> (T. S. Eliot, *The Dry Salvages*)

26. As to that, the long-held hypothesis of the impossibility of "action at a distance" and in-stantaneous "transmission of information" was shown to be wrong, and they were demon-strated to be real events in 1997, albeit the experiments worked with subatomic quanta. Time was shown not to have elapsed, although a measurable, rather considerable space was traversed, if that term can be applied.

27. "Still" meaning "always" in Shakespeare's language.

28. That is, and unless one wishes to see Shakespeare in this play as positing that Macbeth is predestined not to take the path away from darkness and doom. In which case he is antici-pating Jonathan Edwards' awful vision of a sinner in the hands of an angry god. If Macbeth has no choice, then his Lady is someone who has foreseen his path, and only leads him on it in an ancillary way. She does in this resemble a Sibyl, only in a terrible, active form. Her madness and sleeplessness suggest a person who might have been easily recognizable to the ancients, like the witch called Medea, for instance.

29. Tiresias is the ventriloquized narrative voice by which the several voices speak in *The Waste Land* (1922). Eliot calls him "the most important personage in the poem, and says also that "all the women are one woman." Yet he does not tell us why; nor does he tell who she is for him, or who she was in her several pathetic avatars that describe what women are, all forlorn in this famous poem. Far back, a work that stands in its support is the "Pervirgilium

Veneris," which as a Late Latin poem has its roots in the lost traditions Eliot was made aware of by Fraser, Reinach, and Weston, the last being the main source of his imagery, he tells us. It is interesting to note, too, that the poem's epigraph is a quotation from the *Satyricon* of Petronius, and is a chance remark concerning the Cumaean Sibyl hung captive in a cage at Cumae, a city founded by the Greeks in the eighth century B.C. She is mentioned as a valid source by Virgil in the *Aeneid*, where that learned poet treats her with respect. What a comedown from the Sibyl who had reigned at Delphi, to find her sister emanation mocked like this in Nero's day. In the original Latin text Eliot cites, the Sibyl replies in Greek to the adolescents (catamites) who themselves have taunted her in Greek. But Eliot's is an etiolate Tiresias, bleached of substance, a persona that masks nothing, existent only in the words it speaks concerning what has passed, or is passing in his presence, but not of what is to come. Nevertheless, until its closing invocation and whispered prayers, the poem is made up of scenes illustrating representative aspects of failed love between man and woman. This is a Tiresias who seeks expiation even in his spectral form. One may ask, expiation for what crime? He has failed, at the outset, the Hyacinth Girl, the nubile essence of the fertility cult, who glistens with water. Unsurprisingly, from this perspective, the next voice is that of a clairvoyant with a muffled voice, who suffers from "a bad cold," a cold she had caught, doubtless, once upon a time in the Hyacinth garden, where she was accompanied by a silent, impotent, or castrated young man, the young Tiresias as it were. She is now "Madame Sosostris," the "wisest woman in Europe," reading the future from cards, reduced to me-chanical means of foretelling. Being at the end of the end of times, she remains able never-theless to warn Tiresias that he must "fear death by water," which of course was his fate in old age: he drank spring water too cold, which is a figure for "too pure, too original." Tiresias apparently died before the defeat of the Epigoni, of Oedipus' party, so to say, and the victory of Creon, which marks a return to another order of things, an older order, although it has usually been read as the triumph of *Realpolitik* over defiant affirmation of family piety. Sophocles, however, may have regarded Jocasta's brother as the defender of ancient Thebes, whose order belonged rather to the women who served Athena and Artemis and Hera, not male Apollo and Zeus. The thing-in-itself is what cannot be apprehended, either by consciousness or by intuition; likewise, the Riddle of the Sphinx, which was opened by Geza Róheim, is the act of engendering that must not be seen by the child. Hence the "Oedipal complex," which is not a simple matter to deal with at all, in theory or devel-opmentally. It is no accident that the shade of Tiresias is evoked to speak for the despairing poet, since the ancient Tiresias suggests in his person and in myth the link between the sexes, which can alone assure a futurity. Eliot, who had no stake personally in it, and seems to have avoided all possibility until in late middle age he married his secretary, a woman long past childbearing, is a case indeed! One is tempted to muse further as to why his lifelong interest in clairvoyance, or the future, and his struggles from his early studies on to understand time have not been looked into. Why should he have been so attracted to early reconstruction of lost vegetation rites? There are things he never told us and would never tell us about that; and indeed they suggest something that may account for a deflection of some deep anxiety into an anti-Semitism he never renounced in his poetical canon. Perhaps there is a profound, if strange, connection between the rods of Tiresias and Moses, and some unconscious and unknowable resistance to the God of Moses, whose last great priest was perhaps Samuel, the eradicator of "witches." All history is a present story to the poet; to the clairvoyant perhaps that story includes the future, which, coming so often from the woman, has been suppressed from the most ancient times. Róheim's analysis of the Abo-rigine culture offers food for thought in this regard. At any rate, it might be said that the

Wasteland is prophecy looking back in despair. Eliot's career in poetry was ever afterward one of expiation, since there is no forgiveness for such knowledge of what has been lost forever. One might add, the most ancient truth (or way of apprehending Woman) was not so much lost, but as it were struck down by the rod. There is yet more that might be unraveled in this profound poetic memory of a time before time. Aristophanes, to be sure, a comic poet, also told us something in Plato's *Symposium*, when he jested that mankind was a duplex creature in the beginning, and was sundered into man and woman, who are forever trying to rejoin. All our trouble comes from that, since our couplings are fleeting and ephemeral, even if they result in the erection of our lives. Socrates opined that Comedy was a mixed mode, and that we laughed in our tears and wept in our laughter; this small jest of Aristophanes is as close to the essential truth as life itself. Seldom, however, do we rise to its occasion; and there is no laughter to be found in Eliot (*pace* Possum's pussycats, who were a celibate's love). But the Comic is not our concern here.

30. We will inevitably recall that in the competition with Moses the Egyptian wizards were able to turn their rods into serpents, and that he himself was able to start a spring from a barren rock with his staff. Tiresias strikes copulating serpents; with his staff, that is, he hits at the ancient fertility rites of his country of snake cults; and then, after having lived as a woman, punishment intended—by whom, the myth-maker? priestess-deity? deity-priestess? which comes to the same thing—to enlighten him, he repeats the act, the puritanical fellow within him persistent, or else, rather, as echoing some ancient struggle for dominance, and is changed back into a man. Blindness is a trope for castration, as Freud suggested (displacement upward). In one tradition he was blinded (castrated) when he saw Athena bathing. That act would have meant the condign punishment, death, but that his mother was a friend of the goddess. We know that Moses, too, was forbidden to look upon the god at Sinai. What does all this say about women and wisdom and their secrets? *The Bacchae* reveals the horrible punishment for a peeping Tom not protected by a mother's initiation to the female rites. We are peering now into the most remote past through such legends. Yet it is au fond something that Freud glimpsed, as did his students in Europe. The term "repression" must be thought of as having many applications.

31. What was known also about Laius was that, by having been the one to introduce pederasty into Greece, which seems to have been considered an abomination in pre-Attic times, he brought his doom on himself. It was this crime that foredoomed his son Oedipus as well. Such fatalism is it seems the fundamental Greek attitude: Zeus' Law may be iron; yet it is but the expression of the work of the three sisters, Clothos, Lachesis, and Atropos, and all hangs by the thread they work with. Goddesses and human women in the *Odyssey* are introduced to us as sitting before their marvelous looms. It may be that the original model for "the thread" is the umbilical cord.

32. What is intriguing about this matter is that Pelops had been challenged by that king to abduct his daughter, if he would also risk being killed in a chariot pursuit. Thirteen such suitors preceding were all killed by that king, who is said to have wished to be released from the guilt of his incestuous relation to his daughter. Pelops, the fourteenth challenger (cf. note 16 above and the tribute of fourteen sacrificial victims), bribed the stable groom to disable the wheel fastenings, and when the chariot collapsed the king was thrown and himself killed. By cunning and motherwit came that success. The king was Oenomaus of Pisa, a district of Olympia; his daughter was Hippodamia. It seems the king had been warned (by whom? the priestesses of Athena, perhaps?) that he would be killed because of his carnal possession of his daughter. The overthrow of a father who beds his daughter suggests some earlier struggle in ritual form, ritual contests, fertility rites, female concerns,

female needs, and male power. Oedipus himself overthrows his father; there even persists the echo of Pelops' feat, in his pulling the older man from a chariot and killing him. Róheim's study of the Aborigines and his analysis of their practice of subincision offers powerful clues to the pre-history of male anxieties, of which the well-known couvade ritual is but a part.

33. It may be for that reason that Samuel banned witches and sibyls from Israel. Certainly Saul's visit to the Witch of Endor was an act of vain desperation: he was as good as dead, and that is what she foresaw and what she told him. One cannot assume that she had prior intelligence of the situation on the ground, so to say, which seems sometimes to have been the case, indeed very often it was the case, in Delphi. But as for Delphi there remains a large residue of the inexplicable in the prophecies we know of.

34. Perhaps we are all Caliban, and like him hear that our isle, this world, is full of strange music and the invisible comings and goings of unknown beings. It was his mother, an evil woman, who imprisoned in the cleft of a tree that ethereal spirit who, like an angel, has no human feelings. What, we may ask, is the metaphor of that witch, Sycorax, who has such a brutish son as Caliban? Furthermore, why is that unsexed or sexless Ariel caught in a tree's cleft? The masculine protest is quite apparent: were it not for the witch who imprisons a man in a split tree, the male would be all spiritual—so thinks the male, by way of asserting that the female is merely vegetal nature. Perhaps in the end Prospero the Magus is the type of the seer, although scarcely only that, but an active participant in the present affairs of his world. Yet Prospero is but an imagined human being, while it seems that Tiresias may have existed, as the story of his death suggests. Finally, I have met Auntie Vanga, and known another like her. Philosophy has not dreamed, perhaps cannot dream of such beings. In fact, philosophy is not permitted to do so. These matters concern things that came before philosophy, and if one may jest, perhaps they wait to come, here and always, after philosophy.

35. In the non-fatalistic, indeed optimistic Judaic-Christian universe, such persons come as messengers of the Good, like the Elijah of Jewish folklore. I was startled to find the rational Existentialist philosopher Emmanuel Levinas dedicating a word of homage to a strange teacher who appeared to turn his attention to the Talmud—at just such a critical point in his own life, almost as though it were the person of Elijah materializing in historical time and behaving as he does in legend. Cf. Levinas, *Nine Talmudic Readings* (1990).

36. After Sophocles, it was said of Olympias, the mother of Alexander the Macedonian, that she "slept" with snakes, and was so venerated in Macedonia that even when she was defeated in a battle for succession the victors dared not touch her person, so that her execution was carried out by the families of those she had murdered. This was after Euripides had left Athens for Macedon, where he wrote the extraordinary play, *The Bacchae*, which honors Dionysus and his women votaries.

37. Creon, meaning simply "ruler," is so denominated by Sophocles.

38. Male monotheism was not arrived at by mere male fiat. In the Hebrew biblical text she is certainly gone after Abraham. The legends of the Jews are another matter, and foremost we find Lilith, present at the outset, coeval with the creation of Adam. Recent archeological finds tell us more. She is present not only in Canaanite household shrines, but in other physical suggestions that even in the First Temple a female deity perhaps shared power with Yahweh. And, of course, Rachel would not leave behind her household gods, female doubtless, when she left her father's homeland with Jacob, who like his father and grandfather presumably was a Yahweh follower all during nearly two decades he served Laban the Syrian. One wonders about the "maidens," whom she called her "friends," the sorority, that is, of

Jephthah's daughter, who pleaded to spend two months on the hills, in the forest groves with them, lamenting her (unfulfilled) virginity before submitting to be sacrificed by her father in payment to Yahweh for his victory in a crucial battle. There was no tradition of human sacrifice in Israel, certainly not after the redemption of Isaac; rather, a tradition that allowed for the substitution of animals for humans, a tradition that over two millennia gradually altered the proportion of human to animal sacrifices in favor of animal replacements. One may note that Jephthah was himself self-made, the son of a prostitute, as the chronicler has it, and his father was "Gilead," that is, the tribe itself, not necessarily a person. She was his only child, and in a time of polygamy it is perhaps a notable singularity. The story is meant to suggest a deep pathos: for that unfortunate vow was ambiguous. The Yahwists promulgated a very stern god, it seems. It is bemusing to read a contemporary scholiast's assertion that the girl's friends were dedicated Yahwists, women who would grieve with her and still permit such a sacrifice. In any case, Israelite women perpetuated her memory in an annual four-day rite of mourning. Cf. Robert G. Boling, in *Judges: A New Translation with Introduction and Commentary* (1975). Perhaps it may be suggested that the parallel with the earlier sacrifice of Iphigenia by her father Agamemnon in connection with his war aims is striking ("earlier," that is, if the story in Judges is history and the expedition to Troy is history).

39. In a delightful fairy tale recounted by Chaucer's Wife of Bath we read of a young man who was sentenced to death by the Queen—call her Guinevere, say, since that name is derived from that of a chthonic Celtic goddess—for having raped one of her maidens. Rape is perhaps also a metaphor for the imposition of male power. His only reprieve is to find out and bring back the one secret that matters: What does a woman want most of all? Given a year and a day, he only learns the secret in the nick of time from an ancient crone, or hag, whom he promises to marry for having saved his life. That secret is declared clearly at his hearing: Women want most of all the "Maisterie." They wish in short to rule. Alas, they still wish to rule, it might today be said; or, rather, to rule once more. Had Freud but known his Chaucer, he would never have asked his notorious question: What does Woman want? The conclusion of Chaucer's fairy tale, after the young knight's forced marriage to the Loathsome Witch who entered to claim her reward, is as profound as it is charming, and perhaps as important to consider as anything Freud ever proposed on the subject. He might better have asked, "Who was the mother of Tiresias?"

40. It is interesting, too, that when in the *Odyssey* we hear the story of its hero's interviews in Hades it is to the ranks of great women he speaks first, and not to the warriors he knew of yore. Why that litany of ancient female souls, including the name of Jocasta?

41. I once wrote some lines on this theme of the mythical loss of Arcadian innocence:

> Once it had been so simple:
> we walked in a great circle,
> thrice round, and we understood.
> When that circle was broken
> and nothing could hold us back,
> it all changed: now there were stars:
> stars behind stars behind stars.
> (in *After the Armies Have Passed,* 1970, 1998)

Cast

(Before the palace at Thebes, about two generations before the Trojan War. A crowd of children surrounding the priest of Zeus sit suppliant at the altars before the palace of the king. Oedipus comes out and addresses them.)

OEDIPUS

Here, children, you youngest heirs of Cadmus,
what is the meaning of these garlanded
branches of olive? Why does our city
reek with incense and resound with paeans
and the horrid wails of lamentation?
I have come in person—I, Oedipus,
known far and wide, as well as to you all,
my dear children—because I do not care
to hear your troubles from another's lips.
    Stand up, old man, and speak for them! I know   10
your hearts are filled with dread, or you would not
have gathered now to pray like this in fear.

Surely you know that I myself will do
whatever's possible to succor you:
were I made a man of stone, such sorrow
as I see here would have me weep stone tears.

PRIEST

Well then, Oedipus, and our city's king,
we've come to your altars to beseech you,
young and old: some too young to run away,
some hobbled by the burden of their years.   20
I am the priest of Zeus; these children
are tokens of our youth, as yet unwed;
those others, carrying their flowered wreaths,
sit in the market square near Athena's
two temples and the prophesying ashes
of Ismenus. Look around at Thebes,
look at your whole land, storm-tossed and drowning
in the crashing waves of an angry sea.
The fruiting trees are blighted as they bud;
goats, sheep, and cows miscarry as they graze;   30
babies die in the womb and are stillborn;
overhead the ghastly, burning, black god
of the plague flaps its wings and swoops to snatch
away the last of the House of Cadmus,
and Pluton's coffers fill with groans and tears.
   I sit before your hearth with these children,
not because we rank you high as the gods,
though we esteem you first among all men—
both for your knowledge of life, and the strength
you showed when faced by superhuman force.   40
Who but you dared to come to this city
of Cadmus to free us from the tribute
that monstrous singer wrung from our own flesh—
who but you, when Thebes was hopelessly lost!
And that is why it's said, *None but a god
gave you such power to set our lives straight!*

So, Oedipus, we come to you once more:
only the man mightiest in our eyes
will find some means to shield us all from death.
Whether you have heard a god's whispered word,   50
or counsel from some other person's lips,
it's best that wisdom's brought to bear by you.
Come then, greatest of men who walk the earth,
lift this city! Raise up our Thebes from dust!
You, whom we call our hero, preserver,
let not the future say in memory
of your days as king that once you saved us,
but stood aside and watched us as we died.
The happiness you brought us then was crowned
with luck—so may its splendor shine today!   60
It must—if you hope to govern in Thebes
tonight! Or else you're merely sovereign
of a vacant land—what good is a wall
or a ship with not a man to man them?

OEDIPUS
Children, I am truly sorry for you!
How could I not know the need that brings you?
You suffer, yes; but sick as you may be,
not one of you is ill as I am ill!
The pain that strikes you harms you one by one;
but my soul aches for our Thebes, for myself,   70
and yes, for all of you, altogether!
You have not roused me from some drowsy bed;
no, sleepless tears have dragged me out along
the dark and tangled roads of tortured dreams,
until I saw my way: I have sent Creon,
Menoeceus' son Creon, my wife's brother,
to Delphi, to Apollo's halls, to learn
from the Pythia what I must say or do
to halt this city's plunge to utter ruin.
Counting the days since he set out from Thebes,   80

it seems to me that he's been gone too long.
I wonder, is he safe . . . ? When he comes home,
no matter what the god may have advised,
if I do not obey, let me be damned!

PRIEST

Well said! And said in time: Creon's returned.
They're waving to us now: he's on his way.

OEDIPUS

Apollo! Lord! And let him bring good news!
Let his eyes be bright with promising words!

PRIEST

Those leaves that wreathe his head are fresh green bay:
what else could that mean but our salvation?   90

OEDIPUS

We'll soon know—he's close enough to hear me.
Sir, son of Menoeceus, and kinsman!
What answer have you brought us from the god?
(Enter Creon.)

CREON

This message: even trouble at its worst
may be borne—if things take a better turn.

OEDIPUS

Are such words meant to warn or comfort us?
Have you returned with riddles for your pains!

CREON

I would prefer to go inside with you.
It may not suit for all the world to hear.

OEDIPUS

    Speak up! Let people know! I grieve for them   100
    far more than for myself! In god's name, speak!

CREON

    This, then, is what I heard from Apollo.
    This country is corrupt—it's fouled, defiled
    by something we've harbored ourselves. Unless
    we drive it out, we're done for, says the god.

OEDIPUS

    Defiled? By what! And what will cleanse the land?

CREON

    Expulsion. Banishment. Or—execution.
    Murder for murder. Murder is the cause!

OEDIPUS

    And who is the man the god has condemned?

CREON

    Sir, before you became our king in Thebes,   110
    this palace was possessed by Lord Laius.

OEDIPUS

    So they've said. I know the name, not the man.

CREON

    He was killed. The god now clearly tells us,
    His killers must be killed, no matter who!

OEDIPUS

    What! Trace the footsteps of some ancient crime?
    How could I do that? Where would I begin?

CREON

> He's right here in our own land, said the god.
> Seek him; find him; catch him. Or he'll escape.

OEDIPUS

> Where did Laius meet his death? At home?
> In the fields? Or in some other country?   120

CREON

> He left for Delphi. Whether he got there,
> no one knows. He never reached home again.

OEDIPUS

> One clue may lead to other clues. A push
> launches us. It's clear sailing after that.

CREON

> *Ambushed by brigands,* said the god, *and slain.*
> No one man could have put King Laius down.

OEDIPUS

> Who'd have the nerve for it? But—cold, hard cash
> may well have been laid out here in advance.

CREON

> That thought crossed some minds. Still, when Laius died
> not one finger was raised in our behalf.   130

OEDIPUS

> The House of Laius struck by disaster,
> and no one takes a step to solve the crime!

CREON

> The song the Sphinx was singing then was death
> enough for us—we had no time to waste.

OEDIPUS

    I'll take this up and shed some light on your case.
Apollo's right, and you're right: the man's death
demands an answer. For Apollo's sake,
for his, for Thebes', we shall see justice done.
I swear to rid the world of this disease!
And do it—not for some old, far-off friend,   140
but for myself—who knows whether some day
killers might not attempt my life as well?
What helps Laius, helps me—no more, no less.
    Get up, children! Quick! Take your olive poles
away, and call for someone to collect
the people of Cadmus and bring them here.
Let everyone know that Oedipus
will be stopped by nothing. With the god's help,
we must succeed—or else all die like flies!

PRIEST

    Then let us rise, my children. The King's words   150
are words we have hoped to hear a king speak.
May Phoebus who provides these prophecies
now come to stop the plague, and bring us life!
(Exit priest and children; Oedipus and Creon also leave. The Chorus of
       the old men of Thebes takes its place in the
       orchestra and chants the opening ode.)

CHORUS OF THEBAN ELDERS

    Ah, sweet words of Zeus!
What has come to splendid Thebes
from Pytho in golden Delphi?
I'm thrown down, gripped by terror!
I cry to you, O Healer of Delos,
I cry out to you in awe—
What glory will you manifest,   160
what wonder will you bring,
like the new time of a new year?

Tell me now, eternal prophet,
O golden child of golden Hope!
Immortal Athena, daughter of Zeus,
I call on you! And next, on Artemis
your sister, far-famed Artemis,
who sits in the marketplace
and guards our beleaguered land
from her high, round throne, the moon!   170
And upon Apollo too,
whose arrows never fail!
Upon all three, I call!
Come! Show yourselves!
Drive away impending doom,
as once you did when utter ruin
encircled Thebes like a wall of fire!
Return again to hapless Thebes
and bring it succor now!

    Ah, who can name my untold sufferings!   180
Our countrymen lie sick and dying,
and who knows how to stop the march of plague!
Fruit rots, and nothing grows from our lost fields;
though women moan in birth, no infant cries.
Here, there, black shadows flit like dark swallows
towards the shore of the god of the West.

    Ah, who can count their deaths,
so many have been undone,
and the city dying with them as they die!
Children stiffen and shrivel   190
and lie where they were dropped,
but who is there to pity them and weep?
Wives and white-haired mothers
kneel at the row of altars
to lament their loss, and groan in chorus
with those who come to join them in despair.
They raise their voices in ringing prayers
of lamentation to Him, the Healer!

O golden daughter of Zeus,
Show your bright face, and send   200
the light of your protection!
    And let Ares, whose raging roars
scorch our ears—although the brazen clang
of shields be mute—let Ares turn
and leave this land;
let him return to Amphitrite's grotto,
to waves that smash on Thracian shores!
For whatever's left undone at night
will be finished by the end of day.
    Father Zeus, you who flash the lightning's power,   210
destroy him with your thunderbolt!
Lord of Lycia, great Apollo, hear!
I would praise the peerless arrows
you loose from your golden bow
as you stand with us in our defense!
I'd praise the bright torch of Artemis
as she courses the hills of Lycia!
I call on red-cheeked Bacchus,
who named this land,
on gold-capped Bacchus   220
to whom they shout, Io! Io!
Bacchus, friend of Maenads,
let him come to us now,
flourishing his flaring pinewood flambeaux
against Ares, that god who goes
unhonored by all the gods.
(Oedipus returns.)

OEDIPUS
    You've made your demand, and I've heard you out.
    If you intend to listen now to me,
    and act as you must if you're to be healed,
    the cure for all your troubles is at hand.   230
    What I am going to say, I shall say

as one to whom your story comes as news,
as one who knows nothing of that lost time—
although I'd need to find some sort of link
to you, in order to pursue that trail.
Still, I *am* a citizen of this land,
if not by birth. Thus, to all Cadmeans,
I make the following proclamation!
If there should be among you one who knows
how Laius, son of Labdacus, was lost,   240
or by whose hand he died, let him come up!
If death is what he fears should he reveal
the killer's name, this promise I shall keep:
no mark or worse stigma will he suffer,
but safely leave our land—untouched, unharmed.
If the criminal's known to anyone,
a friend or friend's friend, or some foreigner,
let him speak out! I shall be more than grateful:
rewards and gifts from me will fill his arms.
If silence is your choice, because you fear   250
for a friend or for your own weak-kneed self,
and fail to come up boldly now, hear this!
I have revoked your birthright! I forbid
you to join in prayer and sacrifice;
nor shall the holy water touch your lips!
Henceforth you shall be driven from our homes!
Thus says the Pythian voice of the god,
who has made our uncleanness known to me!
      Oedipus joins the fight, he stands beside
the man who was killed, with the god himself.   260
May that murderer, whether he struck
alone or was helped, live a life of hell,
of pure wretchedness, now and forever!
And should I learn he sits at my own hearth,
and yet permit his presence in the house,
may I be cursed myself, may I be doomed
to suffer the fate I've laid on his head!

And all this, I command in the god's name,
for my sake, and for the sake of this land
that lies blasted and burned by angry gods.   270
For even had they not brought down on you
such hell, you should have cleansed yourselves of guilt,
since that great man who was your king had died.
Yes, you should have hunted everywhere!
But, since the power that was his, is mine,
and the woman who had been his, is mine,
and children who might have been his, are mine—
well, only misfortune was left to him,
and that is why I'll fight for King Laius
just as though he had been my own father!   280
Nothing can stop my search for the killer
of the son of Labdacus, descended
from Polydorus, Cadmus before him,
and Agenor, who came here long ago.
As for those who will not help me in this,
may the gods crush their crops beneath their feet,
burn their women dry as bone—let them drop
from this foul plague, or find a fate far worse!
You Cadmeans who second me in this,
I pray that Justice join us in our fight,   290
and that the gods may smile on us like friends.

CHORUS OF THEBAN ELDERS
Since you have made us swear upon our lives,
my lord, I can but speak the simple truth.
I killed no one, nor can I say who did.
Since Phoebus sends to know who bears that guilt,
let Phoebus now reveal the murderer!

OEDIPUS
Agreed. But, when the gods refuse to act,
where is the man alive who can move them?

CHORUS OF THEBAN ELDERS
>May I suggest the next best thing to try?

OEDIPUS
>And if there be a third best, spit it out.   300

CHORUS OF THEBAN ELDERS
>Someone who can see almost as sharply
>as Phoebus himself: the lord Tiresias.
>Truth might well be learned from him—if you'll ask.

OEDIPUS
>And why assume I have not thought of that!
>When Creon counseled it, I sent two men
>to fetch that seer. What can have kept him?

CHORUS OF THEBAN ELDERS
>Of course it's all rumor; old, vague rumor.

OEDIPUS
>What's rumored? I'm open to anything.

CHORUS OF THEBAN ELDERS
>They say that someone killed him on the road.

OEDIPUS
>And so I've heard. But where's that someone now!   310

CHORUS OF THEBAN ELDERS
>If there be but one drop of fear in him,
>he's lost—given the curse you put on him.

OEDIPUS
>Words cannot scare a man who'd kill a king.

CHORUS OF THEBAN ELDERS
> Now we shall know: here comes the only one
> in this world in whom truth lies. From the mouth
> of this prophet, that man will learn his doom.
> *(Enter Tiresias, led by the boy who guides him.)*

OEDIPUS
> Lord Tiresias, master of our lives!
> You who can speak about all things above,
> about whatever moves upon the earth,
> about what men may have revealed to them,   320
> and what cannot be said or understood—
> though blind, you know the deathly blight of Thebes.
> None but you have we found who can protect
> our city and save us from destruction.
> Have you been informed how Phoebus replied
> to our pleadings to free us from this plague?
> He answered: *Find the killers of Laius,*
> *and kill them—or expel them from the land!*
> If birds have carried some message to you,
> then say so; or, if other means lead you   330
> to prophesy, take them, and save yourself
> and the city; save me, and save us all
> from the putrid filth that dead man has sent.
> There is no work greater than this: to use
> your gifts and powers all for mankind's good.

TIRESIAS
> My god, my god! What use is it to know
> what there is to know, when it is useless
> to know it at all! This I understood,
> yet did not. Would I be here, if I had?

OEDIPUS
> Yet you *are* here! What's the matter with you!   340

TIRESIAS

> Send me home! My lot will be lighter there;
> yours more bearable here. Trust me on this.

OEDIPUS

> A fine Theban, to speak such hateful words!
> Withholding information is a crime.

TIRESIAS

> If I am, it's because your aim is wild.
> That's all I need—for you to come at me . . .

OEDIPUS

> Don't turn your face from us, Tiresias!
> We all implore you: Tell us what you know.

TIRESIAS

> You know nothing, none of you! My sorrow
> is mine. Your sorrow's not for me to tell!   350

OEDIPUS

> What! Something evil's here, and you refuse
> to speak its name! Do you intend our deaths?
> You'll let us die! And then you'll ravage Thebes!

TIRESIAS

> Why should I wish to harm myself, or you?
> No more questions. My answers won't make sense.

OEDIPUS

> This is monstrous! Even these stones would crack
> with rage! You say yes—and no; this—and that;
> and yet refuse to say just what you mean.

TIRESIAS

> Listen to him! This man, who cannot hear
> what anger roars in him, accuses me!   360

OEDIPUS

    Insulting words have set my teeth on edge.
    Hemming and hawing. Don't push my patience!

TIRESIAS

    No matter what I may seal in silence,
    things must come to pass . . . as they come to pass.

OEDIPUS

    What must come is what you have come to tell!

TIRESIAS

    You'll get no more from me. I'm done. Rage, rage,
    if you like. I'm done. Rage your worst! Go on!

OEDIPUS

    If that doesn't beat all! Let me tell you
    what *I* think! *I* think that *you've* played a part
    in a plot, and in its execution, too—   370
    even if your hands didn't hold the sword.
    Were you not blind, I'd say that *you* killed him!

TIRESIAS

    Enough! I now demand that you yourself
    obey the order you proclaimed today:
    Never again address these men—or me!
    The pollution of this land comes from you!

OEDIPUS

    Aren't you ashamed to utter such words?
    Do you expect to get away with them?

TIRESIAS

    I'm not! I shall! The truth in me is strong!

OEDIPUS

    A truth you never found in prophecy!   380

TIRESIAS

In fact, it came from you. You had me brought
to Thebes. You made me speak against my will.

OEDIPUS

And such words! Say them once more? But this time,
put them in some way I might understand?

TIRESIAS

Now you're trying to test me! How dare you
pretend my meaning wasn't loud and clear!

OEDIPUS

Come again? It went right past me. Really.

TIRESIAS

I said, *You yourself murdered the man*
whose murderer you say you're looking for!

OEDIPUS

You might be pardoned once for that—but, twice!   390
Abandon all your hopes! Prepare to die!

TIRESIAS

If you believe your blood is boiling now,
you wouldn't care for more such words from me?

OEDIPUS

Waste your breath whatever way can please you.

TIRESIAS

Then hear this! *Your life's a sordid disgrace*
to all you hold your nearest and dearest.
Yet you're so blind you cannot even see
this foul, deadly shambles that you stand in!

OEDIPUS

    While you dare to spew out such calumnies
    and count on creeping home all safe and sound!   400

TIRESIAS

    If truth be my strength, I'm strong. And—I'm free.

OEDIPUS

    Truth may be strong. But you're not strong! You're blind!
    Eyes blind, ears blind, and mind blinder than blind!

TIRESIAS

    How sad it is to hear you throw at me
    the same reproaches all mankind will sling
    against you here in Thebes—and everywhere!

OEDIPUS

    Darkness may protect you. Perhaps. But me—
    and all who see the light—you cannot harm.

TIRESIAS

    Not mine the hand that works to take you down!
    Apollo intends it. His hand will suffice.   410

OEDIPUS

    Creon's come up with this! If not, who then!

TIRESIAS

    Creon's not your problem. Your problem's you!

OEDIPUS

    What's wealth, what's kingship, what's all the craft
    of a life admired for its noble works,
    when hatred's my reward, when the power
    to rule—that royal gift the city gave
    me freely, unasked for—if Creon,

my first friend, if Creon the trustworthy,
has gone behind my back to pitch me out,
set this conniving magician at me,   420
this shrewd swindler who's glimpsed glittering gold,
but who's bat-blind where true vision's concerned.
If you're such a fortune-telling wizard,
how is it you had not a word to say
when Thebes was hounded by that riddling beast?
What wisdom did you offer people then?
No, the secret of her deadly verses
wasn't for the like of you to reveal!
That took true vision by a man of skill,
and it showed you up: neither birds nor gods   430
sent down the knowledge that was needed then.
So, who put a stop to her? Oedipus!
He, who knew nothing, he came—and, bull's-eye!
Had birds informed him? No, his mother wit!
And now you hope to stand behind the throne
of Creon after getting shut of me!
If you and that conspirator assume
you can expel the curse by ridding Thebes
of me, prepare to live to your regret!
If not for the years that weigh that head down—   440
luckily for you—hard knocks would teach you
what it can cost to think treacherous thoughts.

CHORUS OF THEBAN ELDERS

It seems to us that both you, Oedipus,
and this man have been hurling wrathful words,
which is the thing we needed least of all.
The threat we face now is, *What must be done
to carry out the forecast of the god!*

TIRESIAS

King you may be; yet I am not your slave.
Nor am I Creon's, since Loxias owns me.

This fact empowers me to answer you 450
word for word, not only free but equal.
Oh, you may mock me because I am blind.
You have your sight, yes, but what do you see?
Can you perceive your own predicament,
can you discern just where it is you dwell,
or who they are with whom you share your house?
Can you tell us about your origins?
No, you cannot! But I say this to you:
Know first of all: you are the enemy
of people you count as your own—not just 460
those who walk the earth, or those under ground;
next, the curse that stalks like death behind you—
your father's curse, your mother's curse as well—
shall one day drive you helpless from this land.
Now, you may have eyes to see; then, darkness
is all that you will have to contemplate.
Helicon's, Cithaeron's hills and valleys
will echo your cries and lamentations
when you recognize at last the perils
of your marriage, that haven into which 470
you once sailed on such a favoring wind!
And more, worse—things you cannot see as yet—
your children will be wiped out with yourself!
There! Heap abuse on Creon! Mock me now!
No one beneath the sun shall be so torn,
so grimly, from his very life, as you!

OEDIPUS

That I should hear words like these, from this man?
Insufferable! Turn yourself around;
grope your way from my house; and limp on home!
May you be flayed, chopped up, and flung to dogs! 480

TIRESIAS

Would I be here, had you not sent for me?

OEDIPUS

> Would I have let you step into my house,
> had I thought you'd drivel a fool's nonsense!

TIRESIAS

> Yes, a fool, you think, a gibbering fool—
> though those to whom you were born thought me wise.

OEDIPUS

> To whom I was born? Stop! To whom was I born!

TIRESIAS

> You were born today! You perished today!

OEDIPUS

> Riddles! Dark thoughts! Wild words! And wilder threats!

TIRESIAS

> I heard you were the master of riddles?

OEDIPUS

> Fine! Taunt me! Ridicule my splendid feat!   490

TIRESIAS

> Yes! It was that trial which ruined you.

OEDIPUS

> I couldn't care less. Who else would save Thebes?

TIRESIAS

> So that's that! Good! Take me away, boy.

OEDIPUS

> Let him take you, yes. What more can you do
> except to block our way, and pester us!
> Go on and clear out! Take your griefs with you.

TIRESIAS
    I'm going. What I had to say, I've said,
    and you may swear and scowl, for all I care:
    you are not the one who can break me.
    For the last time, this is how things stand here: 500
    The man most wanted for Laius' murder,
    the man you've denounced and threatened with death,
    is to be found nowhere else but in Thebes!
    He's thought to be a stranger in your gates;
    but time will show he's native born to Thebes,
    and little joy will come to him from that—
    because he then shall travel blind, and pick
    and feel his steps before him with a stick.
    And he shall be shown to be a brother
    to his own children, and to his mother   510
    not only a son, but a husband too—
    his mother's lover—and to his father,
    a murderer. Now get yourself inside
    and mull my words; and if you think them false,
    tell the world there is no wisdom in me,
    nor truth in all my empty prophecies!
(Exit Tiresias. Oedipus turns and goes into the palace.)

CHORUS OF THEBAN ELDERS
    Where is the man, who is he
    whom the rock of the oracle
    of Delphi has declaimed
    to have bloodied his hands   520
    in a deed too atrocious
    to be hidden forever?
        The time has come for him
    to flee in fear, faster
    than horses or the winds.
    The son of Zeus himself,
    armed with bolts of fire,
    leaps down like lightning,

followed by the dreadful
shadows of death that never   530
miss their destined mark!
    From the whitecapped peak
of Parnassus, word flamed out:
the world itself was called
to trace the lost footsteps
of that strange and unknown man.
Though he runs through the forests,
through caves, and over rocks,
limping like a sore-lamed bull,
trying to evade the prophecies   540
that rise up from the center
of the earth, they float and soar,
like living forms around him!
    Bitter, bitter, bitter,
the prophet's vexing words!
I cannot believe them,
I cannot deny them,
and cannot call them lies!
Hope lifts me on its wings,
although to past and present   550
I am blind, and see nothing there.
Was there ever contention
between the Labdacids
and the son of Polybus?
If so, it never reached my ears.
Why then should I go up
against the fame of Oedipus,
just to help the Labdacids
hunt down those who caused those deaths?
    Well, mortal affairs are known   560
to all-wise Zeus and Apollo;
but so far as men are concerned,
who says the clairvoyant's words
should carry more weight than mine?

One sort of wisdom may not
serve as well as another.
Unless I see that forecast
realized as clear as day,
I shall never side with those
who fault him—everyone saw   570
how wise he proved himself
when that winged woman
challenged him to risk his life!
The city approved him then;
so why should I judge him now,
and convict him for some crime?
(Enter Creon.)

CREON

Citizens! I have heard myself accused
by King Oedipus of plotting treason,
and I stand before you an angry man.
If he believes that I have injured him   580
in our present fearful situation,
whether by word or deed, what good is life
to me when I hear myself so maligned!
Since I am called a traitor to my friends,
a traitor in your eyes, and a traitor
to the city, it must mean we have reached
a crisis: something dreadful is at hand.

CHORUS OF THEBAN ELDERS

That charge was laid, yes; but he was provoked,
perhaps, to sudden rage. Perhaps it was
not what he meant to say, but forced from him.   590

CREON

Still, it was said, and in so many words,
that the prophet had been counseled by me
to speak such lies and openly, to you!

CHORUS OF THEBAN ELDERS
　　That too, but not deliberately.

CREON
　　Weren't his eyes hard, wasn't his mind cold,
　　when he launched his accusations at me?

CHORUS OF THEBAN ELDERS
　　What rulers do is not for me to judge.
　　But as to him—well, here he is himself.
(Enter Oedipus suddenly.)

OEDIPUS
　　Stop right there! Where do you get such nerve—
　　to show your face at the door of the house　　　　　　600
　　whose master you vilely hoped to murder,
　　and whose kingdom you wished to steal and rule?
　　Let's hear it, if you please: was it a fool
　　you thought you saw in me, or some coward
　　you could push around and dump, just like that?
　　What made you imagine I couldn't see
　　your game, sneaking behind my back that way,
　　or find you out in time to save myself?
　　Aren't you the fool instead, without friends
　　or means, dreaming to snatch at my kingdom,　　　　610
　　when what you want is soldiers and cold cash!

CREON
　　A word to the wise, rather. Just listen
　　to what I have to say to you in turn;
　　hear me out, and try to judge me fairly.

OEDIPUS
　　You're a smooth talker; but I won't hear you,
　　because I know you hate me heart and soul.

CREON

First things first! Try to listen for a change.

OEDIPUS

First things first! Tell me you're not a traitor.

CREON

You're not thinking with your head, if you think
senseless stubbornness to be a virtue.   620

OEDIPUS

And you're not thinking with yours, if you think
to harm your brother and get off unharmed.

CREON

Who could disagree with that? But tell me,
what is all this you say I've done to you?

OEDIPUS

Who talked me into sending someone out
to fetch the venerable prophet here?

CREON

That was my advice, and I stand on it.

OEDIPUS

All right. And when was it that Laius—

CREON

I don't follow you. When did Laius what?

OEDIPUS

Vanish! Struck right off the face of the earth!   630

CREON

That was long years ago. Many long years.

OEDIPUS

> And was the prophet prophesying then?

CREON

> He was just as wise then, and as honored.

OEDIPUS

> And what did have he to say about me?

CREON

> Nothing. Not in my hearing, anyway.

OEDIPUS

> You never hunted down the king's killer?

CREON

> We searched everywhere! Not a trace was found.

OEDIPUS

> Where then was this wise man with his wise words?

CREON

> I don't know. I don't speak when it concerns
> a matter too obscure to comprehend.   640

OEDIPUS

> But *this* you know about. Were you honest,
> you would come clean with me and speak your piece—

CREON

> "*This*"? What is this "*this*"! We'll take it from there.

OEDIPUS

> If you hadn't set up this plot with him,
> would he dare to say that I killed Laius?

CREON

    If that's what he said, who'd know best but you?
    Now, I claim my right to hear from you
    whatever you've just demanded from me!

OEDIPUS

    Whatever! No one calls me murderer!

CREON

    All right. Are you married to my sister?   650

OEDIPUS

    And if I said, "No," who would believe me?

CREON

    And are you not the ruler of this land,
    sharing that power with her equally?

OEDIPUS

    She wants for nothing. What I have is hers.

CREON

    And am I not third, equal to you both?

OEDIPUS

    Yes! Exactly! And there your treason lies!

CREON

    No! Not if you look at things through my eyes.
    Just ask yourself, who would prefer to rule
    afraid of his own shadow, rather than
    govern yet sleep as soundly as a child—   660
    if in each case his power were the same?
    Well, I'm not the fool who wants to be king
    more than I enjoy the royal power
    that I hold—nor would anyone with half

a brain think otherwise. As things now stand,
whatever I need I can have from you,
freely, without worry, and without fear.
Were I king, there are many decisions
I should be forced to make against my will.
Instead, the authority and power   670
I possess are mine to wield as I like,
affording me pleasures denied a king.
No, no, not for me the madness to wish
for more than what pays well and brings honor.
People greet me with smiles; when they want some help
from you, they come to me with their request,
and know that everything, and more, is theirs.
Would I give up all that for just a throne?
A man who thinks things through won't choose evil.
    Well, I don't like that sort of recklessness,   680
and he who risks it cannot count on me.
See for yourself: go to Pytho and ask
if my report about the oracle
checks out; if not, and you discover proof
I plotted crime with that fortune-teller,
condemn me to die, and not by one voice,
but two: your voice and mine—but let's not base
a charge of treason on your mere surmise.
Two things are unjust: to mistake bad men
for good, and to believe a good man bad.   690
What I think is this: drive a true friend out,
and you've lost what most you loved: your own life.
Time will tell, and time will tell you, for sure;
though it takes time to reveal who is just,
who is not—the traitor's known right away.

CHORUS OF THEBAN ELDERS
    Now that was well said, lord. A careful man
    will not trip and fall over his own words;
    but those who think fast think dangerously.

OEDIPUS

    When the plotter makes his move, he moves fast.

    If I sit quietly and wait for him,   700

    I'm caught and done for. Just like that, I'm lost!

CREON

    You want to deport me! That's what you mean!

OEDIPUS

    To live in exile safe? No! I want you dead!

    [at least two lines are missing here]

CREON

    Not until we've seen how jealous you are!

    [another gap in the text here]

OEDIPUS

    So, you don't believe me? You won't give in!

CREON

    What! To a man who denies his friend!

OEDIPUS

    And I deny that you've been true to me.

CREON

    But have you shown yourself as true to me?

OEDIPUS

    True? To a traitor?

CREON

                But you know nothing!

OEDIPUS

    I have to rule.

CREON

                    And this you call ruling!   710

OEDIPUS

    Think of Thebes!

CREON

                    Thebes is mine as well as yours!

CHORUS OF THEBAN ELDERS

    Stop, lords, stop this now! Jocasta's coming!
    Ask her to help you settle your dispute.
    (Jocasta comes out of the house.)

JOCASTA

    You miserable fools! What's wrong with you!
    Fighting in public? Thebes is perishing!
    It's shameful! What's this quarreling about!
    You're puffing up something that means nothing
    to you like a sack of stupid nonsense!
    Come inside, please. And you, Creon, go home!

CREON

    Your husband Oedipus, my sister dear,   720
    has offered me this choice: I am to be
    hounded from my country—or to my death.

OEDIPUS

    Exactly! Why? Because he's laid a plot
    against me—evil, scheming violence.

CREON

    May I not live, but rot and die accursed
    if I've done anything like what you've charged!

JOCASTA

    Oedipus, I implore you, take his word!
    Respect the gods by whom he has sworn.
    Respect me. Respect the men you see here.

CHORUS OF THEBAN ELDERS

    My lord, I beg you! Think! Choose to agree!   730

OEDIPUS

    Say I do. Just what do you want from me?

CHORUS OF THEBAN ELDERS

    Simply to honor this man, this wise man
    whose great oath makes his honor yet greater!

OEDIPUS

    So, you do know what you're asking for!

CHORUS OF THEBAN ELDERS

    Yes!

OEDIPUS

    All right, then! Speak up! Tell me in plain words!

CHORUS OF THEBAN ELDERS

    Your friend has sworn an oath upon his head,
    an oath that makes his life a holy thing.
    How dare you accuse him of bad faith now!
    How dare you deny him his right to speak!   740

OEDIPUS

    You surely know, when you ask me for this,
    you call for my death—or exile from Thebes!

CHORUS OF THEBAN ELDERS

Not so, by the great god, the Sun himself!
May I be abandoned by gods and friends,
may I be horribly destroyed myself,
if such a thought had ever come to me!
Yet my heart is torn apart as I watch
this country waste away! How much worse, then,
if, to all our former troubles, trouble
now be added that comes in fact from you.   750

OEDIPUS

Then let him go. But understand: it means
I'm utterly disgraced, fit for nothing!
So finish me off! Throw me to the dogs!
For your pitiful words, I pity you—
not him! Him I loathe, now and forever!

CREON

It's obvious you give in filled with hatred;
and when you're so enraged, you're dangerous.
A man like you cannot even bear himself.

OEDIPUS

Just go now, and let me be!

CREON

                                        I'm leaving.
You comprehend nothing—they've saved my life.   760

CHORUS OF THEBAN ELDERS

Lady, why do you wait? Take him inside.

JOCASTA

I will—when I have learned what goes on here.

CHORUS OF THEBAN ELDERS
> Something came up, some stupid supposition.
> Still, words can wound, even wild and vague words.

JOCASTA
> On both sides?

CHORUS OF THEBAN ELDERS
> Yes!

JOCASTA
> What were the words they said?

CHORUS OF THEBAN ELDERS
> Enough, enough! Let's leave it now at that.
> I'm far more worried for this country's fate.

OEDIPUS
> At last you've seen this perilous pitfall!
> So much for your subtle judgment! So much
> for blocking my anger, and, what's far worse,   770
> for failing to respect my interests.

CHORUS OF THEBAN ELDERS
> Lord, I've said it before; I'll say it now:
> Should I forget you, think of me as mad!
> Should I forget you—who brought a fine wind
> and saved my country from raging seas—
> call me a fool, an empty-witted fool!

JOCASTA
> Will you, my lord, or will you not explain!
> What can have put you into such a state?

OEDIPUS
> Because I honor you, Lady, far more
> than these, I shall—Creon! and Creon's plot!   780

JOCASTA

> Will you make sense of this quarrel to me?

OEDIPUS

> He says I killed Laius. No more, no less.

JOCASTA

> And where did he get such information?
> Or is it something that he knows himself?

OEDIPUS

> You can be sure he keeps his own mouth clean.
> No, for this he brought a foul prophet in.

JOCASTA

> Just drop that subject altogether now.
> Take it from me: there is nothing mortal
> that can see with the eyes of a prophet.
> I'll show you proof in a very few words.   790
> Once upon a time, an oracle reached
> Laius—I won't say it came from Phoebus
> himself, but through his servants—and it said,
> *You are doomed to die by your own son's hand*—
> the child that I should one day bear to him.
> The story has it that foreign brigands
> murdered him at the crossing of three roads.
> But—when our child was only three days old,
> Laius pinned his ankles and had him tossed
> away somewhere upon a mountainside.   800
> So it wasn't Apollo that arranged
> things to make him his father's murderer;
> nor was Laius the victim of the fate
> he feared: death at the hand of his own son.
> So much for voices prophesying doom!
> Pay them no attention. I tell you this:

When the god wants some thing, he'll hunt, he'll find,
and reveal it when and as he pleases.

OEDIPUS

O, Lady, how strange! Listening to you,
I seemed suddenly somewhere else, and lost,   810
as though my thoughts were turning round and round.

JOCASTA

What next! Why do you look at me like that?

OEDIPUS

Did I hear you say, three roads meet somewhere,
and that Laius was butchered at that place!

JOCASTA

So the tale went then; so it goes today.

OEDIPUS

And that calamity fell on him—where?

JOCASTA

Phocis. The road forks there. Whether you go
from Delphi or Daulis, you reach Phocis.

OEDIPUS

And that all happened just how long ago?

JOCASTA

It was announced in Thebes a little while   820
before you showed up—and became our king.

OEDIPUS

O Zeus! Have you judged me—and condemned me?

JOCASTA

> Why should that upset you so, Oedipus?

OEDIPUS

> Not yet; not yet.   How old a man was he?
> Laius, I mean. And what did he look like?

JOCASTA

> His hair was still black, but starting to gray;
> in fact, he looked a little like yourself.

OEDIPUS

> O my god! It begins to seem as though
> I have myself condemned and damned myself.

JOCASTA

> To hear you talk that way fills me with dread.   830

OEDIPUS

> I fear the prophet may not be so blind.
> He sees in darkness. Light may come from you!

JOCASTA

> You frighten me! What's known is all I know.

OEDIPUS

> Was he heavily guarded, like a king,
> or did he travel lightly and alone?

JOCASTA

> Five in all. His herald made one of them.
> Laius rode by himself in a wagon.

OEDIPUS

> It's clear as crystal now! God in heaven!
> Lady, where did you get this story from?

JOCASTA

    A slave told me. The only one who lived.   840

OEDIPUS

    Would he happen to be here in this house?

JOCASTA

    No. After making his way home at last,
    he found you on the throne. Laius was dead.
    He took my hand and pleaded to be sent
    from Thebes to outlying pastures and fields,
    as far as possible from our city.
    And I let him go because he was good,
    and deserved fair treatment, not a whipping.

OEDIPUS

    What do you think, can he be brought back soon?

JOCASTA

    I don't see why not; but whatever for?   850

OEDIPUS

    Chances are I've said much too much by now.
    I need to see him. I have my reasons.

JOCASTA

    In that case, he'll come. Still, my lord, I think
    you ought to let me know what worries you.

OEDIPUS

    Though I'm stretched tight as a bowstring, Lady,
    it's not something I would hold back from you.
    Besides, who but yourself should be the first
    to hear my story, since it seems my fate
    subjects me to such damnable torment!

Polybus of Corinth was my father,   860
a Dorian my mother, Merope;
they raised me as the greatest citizen
of Corinth—till something happened,
a bizarre, incredible incident—
Whoever could imagine such a thing!
    One night a man—some dinner guest, blind drunk—
declared that I was not my father's son.
I was beside myself, yet held my rage
till morning, when I went to my mother
and father and asked, What was *that* about?   870
My parents took good care to pay him back
for his insulting words. And that was that,
they thought: my anger had been assuaged.
Still, his mockery lingered and vexed me.
In the end I went to Pytho, alone,
only to be sent away without help—
I was cheated there, and scorned by Phoebus,
who told me the most sad and awful things
about myself: that I would bed my mother
and get from her a brood the world would shun;   880
and worse, that I should be the murderer
of the very man who'd begotten me!
    Hearing this, I left Corinth behind me
forever; guided by the stars, I marched
straight ahead, so as to prevent the shame
predicted by those cruel oracles.
And here's what happened, Lady—it's all true!
One day as I went walking past a place
where three roads cross, a herald met me,
followed by a wagon like the wagon   890
you mentioned, and in it there rode a man.
Not only did his officious servant
attempt to drive me from my way by force,
but that old man himself howled rude commands.

And his driver so enraged me, that when
he ran me down, I lashed right out at him.
Then, seeing what I had done, the old man
waited till I walked by his chariot,
and crowned me with his two-bladed ox-goad.
That blow I paid back, but with interest!   900
My hand held my walking stick, and my stick
struck his head: he fell back, stunned, and tumbled,
from that cart like a sack. I killed them all.
If that foreigner was in any way
connected with Laius, then who could be
more miserable than I, more hateful
to the gods—a man henceforth unwelcome
to the stranger's home or the citizen's;
a man never to be greeted, but chased
away from every house in this land!   910
And who else was it if not I myself
alone who laid these curses on my head?
Am I the one who fouls a dead man's bed
with these hands—the same hands that murdered him?
Am I then so utterly unholy,
so criminal that I must leave my land,
exiled, never to see the dear faces
of those I love, never again to set
my foot upon my native soil—or else
fated to marry my mother, and kill   920
Polybus my father, the man who gave
me life and raised me up as his good son?
Would it be wrong to think that some cruel
divinity had made these moves for me?
May I never live to see such a day!
Never, by the sacred light of the gods!
may I behold such a calamity's
horrendous sight! May I instead be lost
from all that good men honor and respect!

CHORUS OF THEBAN ELDERS

> This is too horrible for us, my lord!   930
> Yet we see hope for you! Until you've heard
> that man's own story, hope is left for you!

OEDIPUS

> Hope, is it! There is just hope enough left
> to hold me while I await that herdsman!

JOCASTA

> But, once he's here, what would you hope to do?

OEDIPUS

> It's very simple: if it should turn out
> he says what you've said, then I'm a free man!

JOCASTA

> And what, exactly, did you hear me say?

OEDIPUS

> That brigands killed him. Therefore, if he says
> it was brigands, it means he was not killed   940
> by me—since brigands are not one but more.
> But if he tells us there was but one man—
> one man alone—the finger points at me.

JOCASTA

> Now listen: that's the way we had the news;
> so why should he take his story back now,
> since the whole city heard it from him then,
> not only myself. Though, say, he retracts—
> how can it be proved that Laius was killed
> as it was foretold, that Loxias meant
> he was the one to die at my son's hand?   950
> A piteous infant who had perished
> years long past—how could that child have killed him?

After that, what were warnings worth to me?
So much for signs, and all your prophecies!

OEDIPUS

Which makes good sense. Still, send out for that slave,
and make sure your summons will be obeyed.

JOCASTA

Said, and done: I'll have him called back. I can
deny you nothing. Come now, let's go in.
(*Exit Oedipus and Jocasta.*)

CHORUS OF THEBAN ELDERS

May I win praise for purity
and reverence in word and deed;   960
may I be blessed by destiny
to speak and act according
to the high laws that heaven makes,
whose one father is Olympus!
Mortal mankind never made them;
mortal sleep cannot forget them!
For in those laws the great god lives,
and he remains forever young.
　　The tyrant is the scornful child
of scornful insolence—let that tyrant   970
feast on vanity, and on excess
unseemly and wrong, let him climb
as high as the crown of the temple;
yet from thence he shall be forced
to leap into the tightest net,
from whose mesh there's no escape.
Still, I beseech the god: preserve
his wrestler's knotted hold that brought
our city its salvation once—
the god who is our lord and shield.   980
Him I trust, now and forever.

As for that man whose words and deeds
are arrogant, who fears not justice,
and scorns the places of the gods,
who takes unfair advantage,
who walks without due reverence,
and lays his hands on sacred things—
may he be driven to his doom!
Such a man cannot resist
the fiery shafts of passion—   990
were we to honor him,
how could we offer then
our dances to the gods?
  Should these oracles prove false,
should believers lose their faith
in prophecy, no pilgrimage
to the perfect navel of the world,
nor to the temple at Abae,
nor to Olympia's pure shrine,
shall stain my sandals with its dust!   1000
But, O Ruler!—if they are right
to call you Ruler, Lord of All,
Zeus!—let your eternal might
remember what I have to say!
The oracles of Laius
have faded from men's memories,
wiped clean away by time;
Apollo nowhere shows himself
to us in glory; and the power
of the gods is now as nothing.   1010

(Jocasta enters, carrying offerings to be presented to the statue of Apollo that stands onstage.)

JOCASTA

Lords of the land, the time has come for me
to do what is best: to turn to the gods

and present these garlands with this incense
to their shrines. The griefs with which Oedipus
inflames his mind have so unbalanced him,
that he confuses causes with effects:
he fails to think like a rational man,
but is swayed by anyone who tells him
tales of terrors past and terrors to come.
Since I have tried in vain to counsel him,　　　　　　1020
I must turn to you in supplication,
Apollo of Lycia, as our neighbor.
With my prayers, I offer you these gifts,
and hope to have from you some remedy
to cleanse us all of errors and misdeeds.
To see the captain of our ship like this—
paralyzed—fills us with fear for ourselves.
(Enter Messenger.)

MESSENGER

Can someone here tell me how I can find
the house of King Oedipus? Better yet,
does anyone know where the king might be?　　　　　1030

CHORUS OF THEBAN ELDERS

That's his house, stranger. You'll find him at home.
And the lady standing there before you
has been his children's mother and his wife.

MESSENGER

Since she is his queen, let her be happy!
Happy as those who are always happy!

JOCASTA

So may you, stranger, for your courtesy
alone deserves it! Now, what is your wish,
or have you come to Thebes to bring us news?

MESSENGER

>Lady, for your house, and for your husband,
>my message is one that must give you joy!   1040

JOCASTA

>If so, what is it? Where do you come from?

MESSENGER

>From Corinth. What I have to say will please—
>yes!—but then, it may sadden you as well.

JOCASTA

>Is good news bad news? How can that be so?

MESSENGER

>The Isthmian folk intend to crown him
>as their king—or so runs the story there.

JOCASTA

>King? Then old Polybus rules them no more?

MESSENGER

>No more. He's now a prisoner of Death.

JOCASTA

>Dead, you say! The father of Oedipus?

MESSENGER

>In plain words, yes. If I lie, have me killed.   1050

JOCASTA

>You, slave! Go in, give the master this news!
>Ah, you gods! You and all your prophecies!
>Where are you now! This was the man you feared,
>Oedipus! The man from whose house you fled
>to keep your hands clean has died in his bed!
>
>*(Enter Oedipus.)*

OEDIPUS

    Jocasta, dearest heart, what is it now?
    Why have I been called from the house like this!

JOCASTA

    I'd like you to listen to this man's tale,
    and tell me just what the god's oracles—
    the god's precious oracles!—are good for.   1060

OEDIPUS

    Who's he? And what has he to say to me?

JOCASTA

    He comes from Corinth. He brings this report:
    your father is dead. Polybus is dead.

OEDIPUS

    What is this, stranger! In your own words, please!

MESSENGER

    If I must be the one to tell you first—
    it's absolutely true: he's dead and gone!

OEDIPUS

    Treason? He was betrayed! Or was he sick?

MESSENGER

    What does it take to put old folks to sleep?

OEDIPUS

    Then illness was what killed him? A pity.

MESSENGER

    And the many years of a long life, too.   1070

OEDIPUS

> So, Lady! So . . . ! And we knelt at Delphi's
> fiery footstool, or stared at birds
> who croaked prophetic messages on high
> that said my father's doom would come from me!
> But now my father lies deep in his tomb—
> and here I stand, no weapon in my hand—
> unless he perished longing to see me . . . ?
> and that's all the blame I'll bear for his death.
> Well, Hades holds him, and with Polybus
> have gone those oracles that oppressed us—   1080
> worth nothing now; worth less than nothing now.

JOCASTA

> How long since I predicted this to you?

OEDIPUS

> You did, you did. But fear rose and seized me.

JOCASTA

> What's come of it? Nothing! What worries you?

OEDIPUS

> Sleep with my mother?! That's frightful enough!

JOCASTA

> Can a man live in constant fear like this?
> Since he knows he knows nothing of his fate,
> should he not be ruled by what is the case?
> It's better to make the best of each day;
> but—to worry you'll marry your mother!   1090
> So many men have slept with their mothers,
> and made love to them as well—in their dreams!
> The man who knows such dreams are merely dreams
> can best confront his life, and bear it too.

OEDIPUS

Fine words, and even true—but for one fact:
my mother's still alive. And while she lives,
although you may be right, I am afraid.

JOCASTA

Yet your father's funeral sheds great light . . .

OEDIPUS

Yes, of course—still, while *she* remains alive . . .

MESSENGER

Who is this woman who scares you like this?   1100

OEDIPUS

Polybus' widow, old man. Merope.

MESSENGER

And what's so dreadful about the lady?

OEDIPUS

Stranger, the gods sent down some ghastly words.

MESSENGER

Such as? Or are they not for ears like mine?

OEDIPUS

And why not? Loxias once said that I
was destined to bed my mother, and spill
my father's blood with these two hands of mine.
Because of that I left home and Corinth
long ago to find my fortune elsewhere,
forgoing one of life's sweetest pleasures: 1110
the sight of my parents' loving faces.

MESSENGER

And that was the fear that drove you away?

OEDIPUS

Yes, old man, of course! So as not to be
my father's murderer—it haunted me!

MESSENGER

My lord, my journey here to you was made
in friendship. Let me free you from this fear?

OEDIPUS

Rich would be a poor word for your reward.

MESSENGER

What brought me was that hope! May I be frank?
For just a little something thrown my way—
if you returned—went home—because of me . . . ?   1120

OEDIPUS

What! Set foot once more in my parents' house!

MESSENGER

Ah, my son, it's as plain as plain can be:
you haven't a clue to what you're about.

OEDIPUS

What's this! You'd better make it clear! Be quick!

MESSENGER

If that's all that blocks the road to Corinth . . . ?

OEDIPUS

And that Phoebus may have spoken truly.

MESSENGER
> Pollution from your parents frightens you?

OEDIPUS
> That, and that alone, old man. Nothing else.

MESSENGER
> Then it's last thing in the whole world to make
> you lose your sleep. It's strange you don't know that.   1130

OEDIPUS
> Stranger still were I not to fear for them!

MESSENGER
> What's Polybus to you, or you to him!

OEDIPUS
> Are you suggesting he's not my father!

MESSENGER
> If he's your father, I'm your father too!

OEDIPUS
> And who are you to me? No one at all!

MESSENGER
> Did I sire you? Well, then! Neither did he.

OEDIPUS
> He called me son! Why should he call me son?

MESSENGER
> From these two hands he had you as a gift.

OEDIPUS
> And on this gift he lavished so much love?

MESSENGER

    To that he'd come, long childless as he was.   1140

OEDIPUS

    Did you buy me? How did I come to you?

MESSENGER

    I found you in a glen in Cithaeron.

OEDIPUS

    And what took you to those mountain forests?

MESSENGER

    I kept watch over flocks pastured up there.

OEDIPUS

    Serving time as a wandering shepherd?

MESSENGER

    So it was, my son, when I saved your life.

OEDIPUS

    When you found me and took me in your arms,
    what was my condition? What was wrong with me?

MESSENGER

    As to that, your ankles tell the whole tale.

OEDIPUS

    Ach! Why bring back that ancient misery?   1150

MESSENGER

    I cut the rope to which you had been staked.
    It was sad—your ankles had been pierced.

OEDIPUS

    I was marked from the cradle by that shame!

MESSENGER
> And that's how you got the name you're known by.

OEDIPUS
> Who called me that, by god! Did my father
> or my mother name me? Speak up, old man!

MESSENGER
> As to that, I don't know. The man who knew
> it all was the man who gave you to me.

OEDIPUS
> So then, you *weren't* the one who found me!
> You just received me from somebody else?   1160

MESSENGER
> As to that, it was another shepherd.

OEDIPUS
> All right, who was he? Can't you tell the truth!

MESSENGER
> I think they said he belonged to Laius.

OEDIPUS
> The one who ruled here once upon a time?

MESSENGER
> As to that, well, yes: his shepherd he was.

OEDIPUS
> I want to see this man! Is he alive?

MESSENGER
> Who better than your countrymen should know?

OEDIPUS

>Is there someone among you standing here
>who knows the shepherd this man has described?
>Has he been seen in the fields, or in town?   1170
>Speak up! This must be straightened out right now!

CHORUS OF THEBAN ELDERS

>That should be the man you wanted to see,
>that fellow from the fields—but Jocasta
>is certainly the one that knows who's meant.

OEDIPUS

>You recall the man we sent for, Lady.
>Is he the same fellow this man's described?

JOCASTA

>It doesn't matter if he is or not.
>Don't give it a thought! Just let his words go!

OEDIPUS

>What! Now that we've heard all these hints and clues,
>I'm to stop my birth from coming to light!   1180

JOCASTA

>Do you value your life? Drop these questions!
>My suffering suffices for us both!

OEDIPUS

>What are you worried for? Suppose I am
>the child of slaves who were children of slaves
>born to slaves—that won't make a slave of you!

JOCASTA

>Listen to me! Enough's enough! Stop, I say!

OEDIPUS

    You'd prefer me to live my life a lie!

JOCASTA

    My wish is for what's truly best for you.

OEDIPUS

    And for years I've been oppressed by that "best"!

JOCASTA

    Wretch! I hope you never learn who you are!   1190

OEDIPUS

    Won't someone go and bring that shepherd here?
    Pride may well suit *her* noble family . . . !

JOCASTA

    Ah, you miserable man, you! What's left
    for me to say! Nothing! Nothing! Nothing!
(Exit Jocasta.)

CHORUS OF THEBAN ELDERS

    Lord Oedipus, your lady's run away
    in bitter anguish. From silence and grief
    I fear some evil surely must explode.

OEDIPUS

    Let it! Let it! Come what may, I must know
    my origins, were they lower than low.
    She's a woman, proud as women are proud;   1200
    she's shamed to think that I'm ignobly born.
    But I am fortune's child—my mother was
    that great event that brought me here and made
    me king! So no one can dishonor me.
    That was my true mother, and all the years

since then made me what I am—whether great
or small—they alone stand for next of kin.
How could I now, with such a birth as that,
become another sort of man—a man
who fears to learn who gave his life to him!   1210
(Oedipus remains onstage during the third choral song.)

CHORUS OF THEBAN ELDERS
    If a seer be what I am,
and one who judges wisely,
then, O Cithaeron, you shall
see tomorrow's moon at the full,
and know yourself in glory
as one and the same kinsman—
as the nurse, and mother, too,
of Oedipus! With dances
shall we honor you, for kind
to our princes you have been!   1220
Now, O Phoebus, hear our cries!
And let these things please your eyes!
    Who was it gave you birth,
who, among those who live long,
who took Pan as your father,
Pan who wanders the mountains?
Could it have been some bedmate
of Loxias, who loves high pastures?
Or else the lord of Cyllene,
or some god like the Bacchus   1230
whose home is upon the peaks,
and had you as love gift
from one of those dark-eyed Nymphs
with whom he likes to dally?

OEDIPUS
    If I may trust my eyes, honored sirs,
I would guess they see the very shepherd

we sent for. Though I've never seen the man,
he's old enough to be the one we want;
and, yes, those servants bringing him are mine.
If Laius held him in his service once,   1240
who else would recognize him, if not you?

CHORUS OF THEBAN ELDERS
    Of course I know him! And shepherd he is;
    a loyal servant of Laius as well.
(Enter Shepherd.)

OEDIPUS
    You, Corinthian! I ask you, stranger:
    Is this the man you meant?

MESSENGER
                            The one you see.

OEDIPUS
    Look at me, old man! Answer when I speak!
    Was Laius once your master in this house?

SHEPHERD
    They raised me here. I was no boughten slave.

OEDIPUS
    What sort of work was it you had to do?

SHEPHERD
    All my days have been passed as a herdsman.   1250

OEDIPUS
    And where did you use to set up shelter?

SHEPHERD
    Cithaeron mostly. Around there. Those parts.

OEDIPUS

So you know this man? You've met him before?

SHEPHERD

Who? What sort of man should I meet out there?

OEDIPUS

This sort! You once had dealings with this man!

SHEPHERD

Who, me? With him? Not that I would recall.

MESSENGER

So he says, my lord! Though he may deny,
trust me, I'll bring it back to him! He knows
that when we pitched our camp on Cithaeron
he tended two herds, while I had but one.   1260
In those days we trudged together, six months
at a time for three whole seasons, from Spring
until Arcturus rose up in our skies.
When winter's blast drove me down with my flock,
he took his off to their pens with Laius.
That's all forgotten, geezer? True? Or false!

SHEPHERD

True, true. But then, that was so long ago.

MESSENGER

You gave me a baby—*that*, you'd recall!
A child to raise as though it was my own?

SHEPHERD

You had a *child* from *me*? What's *this* about?   1270

MESSENGER

That man, sir, was in fact that same child.

SHEPHERD

Bite your tongue! May plague rot you to your bones!

OEDIPUS

Drop your stick, old man! Drop, I say! Such oaths
will earn you blows far worse than you'll give him!

SHEPHERD

Why, most noble lord? What wrong have I done?

OEDIPUS

Not one word have you said about that child!

SHEPHERD

What does he know! He's wasting your good time.

OEDIPUS

If kind words won't work, pain can make you talk.

SHEPHERD

I'm old! Don't torture me! I'm an old man!

OEDIPUS

Hold him, you! Tie his old arms behind him!   1280

SHEPHERD

Ah, ah, why hit on me! What's there to learn?

OEDIPUS

Did you bring this man a child? Yes? Or no!

SHEPHERD

Better for me I should have died that day!

OEDIPUS

Die you shall. Here and now. So tell the truth!

SHEPHERD
    I'm damned if I don't, and damned if I do.

OEDIPUS
    Why this song and dance? What will it get you?

SHEPHERD
    As I said before—I gave him the child!

OEDIPUS
    Was it yours? Or whose? Where did you find it?

SHEPHERD
    No, it wasn't mine. It was brought to me.

OEDIPUS
    By someone here? Who was it? From which house?   1290

SHEPHERD
    Please, Lord, no more questions! I can't go on.

OEDIPUS
    If I have to ask you again—you're dead!

SHEPHERD
    That poor child came from the house of Laius.

OEDIPUS
    A slave's child? Or from his own family?

SHEPHERD
    My tale's now come to a treacherous turn.

OEDIPUS
    I don't like the sound of that. Go on, talk!

SHEPHERD

    It was thought to belong to King Laius.
    Your wife's the one to say how things then stood.

OEDIPUS

    Who left the child with you?

SHEPHERD

                    She did, my lord.

OEDIPUS

    She herself? But why?

SHEPHERD

             To be rid of it.   1300

OEDIPUS

    Poor thing! Hers, was it?

SHEPHERD

            Doomed, they said. Poor thing!

OEDIPUS

    How, doomed?

SHEPHERD

         To kill his father and mother.

OEDIPUS

    And you handed such a creature to him!

SHEPHERD

    My heart bled for it. Lord, I thought, surely,
    surely he'd take it far away from here.
    Instead, he saved it . . . for catastrophe—
    because, if you're the man he claims you are,
    then you were born to live in agony!

OEDIPUS

    Ah, me! I see it all! Great god, I see!

    I see, clear as day! Never shall I see   1310

    again by such light! Damned when I was born!

    Damned when I killed! And when I married, damned!

(Exit Oedipus; exit messenger and shepherd.)

CHORUS OF THEBAN ELDERS

    What are you, Children of Men?

    How close to nothingness you are!

    You think you may live to know

    some happiness for yourselves,

    enough to taste its sweetness

    before you go forever.

        Yet look at poor Oedipus

    and tell me, am I wrong   1320

    to say, This man's misery

    reminds us one and all:

    nothing human can be worth

    desiring—or envying!

    Your deadly arrow it was, O Zeus!

    pierced the prophetic heart

    of that eagle-clawed virgin—

    against all the odds—

    and marked him for triumph—

    a triumph not altogether   1330

    pleasing to the gods,

    even though his victory

    saved us from slaughter

    and her murdering songs.

    For that feat, we honored him;

    for that feat, we called him king;

    and for that feat, we offered him

    the throne of mighty Thebes.

        But now, whose torments are worse

    and who must suffer such a life   1340

as his, so debased, so sad
it tells us all our tears are lost.
Ah, this is fame! Ah, Oedipus!
To have entered that port twice,
the same wide, welcoming port—
first as child, then as father—
and both upon your wedding night!
And how, how could the same field
your father plowed before you
give you fruit—yet still be silent!   1350
    Whatever there is to see
in this world, time sees it all.
What was thought so secret
was cursed, condemned,
and sentenced long ago:
a marriage monstrous
for you, for your children,
and for many men to come!
If only, son of Laius,
my eyes had never seen you!   1360
Ah, ah, if only! Lament!
Lament! Lament! This dirge
must weep its tears for all of us!
In the end what's left is truth:
though you restored our lives,
you dulled our eyes with death!
(*Enter Second Messenger.*)

SECOND MESSENGER
    Most honored of all honored in this land—
    if still you honor the house of Laius—
    you must hear things too horrible to hear,
    you must see things too sinister to see!   1370
    Prepare to mourn griefs too mournful to mourn!
    This house of hidden horrors—of horrors
    not chosen, yet not unchosen—horrors

coming now to light for the world to see:
such horrors that not the Danube river
nor the Phasis in flood could scour clean.
Yet the worst grief of all must be the grief—
unwilled or willed—we bring upon ourselves.

CHORUS OF THEBAN ELDERS
We know of far too many grievous things.
What new grief will you pour upon our heads?   1380

SECOND MESSENGER
I'll say first what you first should learn from me:
Jocasta, royal Jocasta, is dead.

CHORUS OF THEBAN ELDERS
Sad words, saddest of words! How did she die?

SECOND MESSENGER
She killed herself. Though you are fortunate
to have been spared such a terrible sight—
that wretched woman's wretched sufferings!—
what I have pieced together must be heard.
In her passion, she pushed through those portals
and fled in fury to her bridal bed,
madly tearing with both hands at her hair.   1390
Laius! she wailed, *Laius!* as she slammed shut
her bedroom doors, and cried out to his corpse
how she recalled their making love on it
so long ago—the love that brought him death
and let her live condemned to bear a brood
to his own atrocious son! She sobbed and wept
upon that bed, where twice in suffering
she'd brought forth: a husband by her husband,
and children by her own child. How she died
after that is something I do not know;   1400
because then Oedipus broke in, and roared

out so, we feared to look at her until
she'd reached her calamitous conclusion—
but stared at him, raging back and forth,
shouting for someone to hand him a sword,
never asking for his wife, but, instead,
demanding to be taken to the field
that had produced not just one, but two crops—
himself the first, his children next by him!
And as he raved to us and at the walls,   1410
some god revealed Jocasta then to him—
it was none of *our* doing!—and he rushed—
it seemed like he was being rudely shoved—
howling gruesomely at those double doors,
and smashed their bolts right out of their sockets,
and stumbled into the room. We caught sight
of her body hanging there: the woman
had twisted a noose tight around her neck.
What a frightful bellow that madman gave
as he stared at her, and fumbled at the knot   1420
from which she hung—but what we saw happen
once he'd laid that poor creature on the stones
was grisly to behold. He broke apart
the golden brooches that adorned her robe,
and lifting his face, struck at his eyes,
swearing words to this effect: *Never*
should they look again at such desolation,
and such appalling deeds as had been his!
From this day on, they would see in blackness
all that should never have been seen at all,   1430
though they had failed to see and recognize
what ought to have been known and understood!
Over and over he muttered these oaths;
again and again he stabbed at his eyes,
those bloodied eyeballs dripping gore that soaked
his cheeks—when suddenly a shower of blood
came bursting down like black hail, like the grief

that was their horror—man's and woman's both.
They had been happy once, true happiness
that now was lamentation, ruin, shame,   1440
and death—not one of all the miseries
that can be named was missing from their fates.

CHORUS OF THEBAN ELDERS
    Is there any balm for that wild man's pain?

SECOND MESSENGER
    He's begging someone to unbar the gates—
    Let Cadmeans all gaze upon this wretch!
    See the patricide, see the matricide—
    and shouting words too blasphemous for me
    to dare repeat. "This house is cursed," he shouts
    and he himself condemned himself as well!
    He means to cast himself out of this land.   1450
    He needs some guide, though, a guide strong enough
    to help him bear the sickness of his life.
    The gates have been unbarred. And now you'll see
    a sight to make whoever hates him weep.
(*Enter Oedipus, blinded now.*)

CHORUS OF THEBAN ELDERS
    What grief, what grief! O, what grief!
    Such grief as I have never seen!
    Grief too frightening to see!
    Miserable, maddened man,
    what has happened to you?
    Who can be the god that pounced,   1460
    that leapt upon your sad life
    with a leap as long as doom?
    Poor man! Poor man! Poor, poor man!
    Who can bear to see you now!
 · Though questions remain unasked,
    and questions remain unanswered—

so many riddles to unravel—
the dread you fill me with
makes me wish to know it all!

OEDIPUS

Ah me! Wretched, wretched me!   1470
Where does my anguish lead?
What wind blows my voice where?
Ah, God! How far have you flown!

CHORUS OF THEBAN ELDERS

To something, somewhere. Whatever it is,
it never must be heard, and never seen!

OEDIPUS

Ah, ah, what a fog of filthy darkness
is blowing on some evil wind! Ai, me!
It's coming on, it's shrouding me! Ai, me!
Indescribable! Irresistible!
It stings and goads me with the memory   1480
of all my troubles, and my grief and pain!

CHORUS OF THEBAN ELDERS

With woes like yours, these bloody tears, these cries
and lamentations may be forgiven.

OEDIPUS

Are you still there, my friend, to keep me from harm?
Will you remain to care for this blind man?
Ai, me! Ai, me! Though I'm lost in darkness,
I can tell you're there! Yes! I know your voice!

CHORUS OF THEBAN ELDERS

Horrid! How could you do this to yourself!
What god drove you to wreck your sight!

OEDIPUS

It was Apollo, dear friends! Apollo,   1490
who brought about this cruel agony!
The hand that struck my eyes was mine alone!
What is there in the world for me to see,
if there is nothing to look at with joy!

CHORUS OF THEBAN ELDERS

What you've said is true. Sadly, sadly true.

OEDIPUS

What is left for me to look at with love?
Whose greeting would be music to these ears,
I ask you! So, take me away, dear friends,
take me with you, friends, as soon as you can—
take this damned one, three times damned and done for!   1500
What man on earth's more hated by the gods!

CHORUS OF THEBAN ELDERS

Miserable in mind! Miserable
in misfortune! Never to have known you!
How I wish I'd never come to know you!

OEDIPUS

May God curse that shepherd who cut those cords
from my feet and saved me—to let me live!
What kind of kindness was that? Had I died,
I'd not have brought such grief upon myself,
and this sorrow would have been spared my friends.

CHORUS OF THEBAN ELDERS

How it hurts to say, *So it should have been!*   1510

OEDIPUS

Because I would not then have come to kill
my father, only to be called the groom

of the bride who had given birth to me.
God-forsaken! Child of unblessed parents!
Partaker of my father's marriage bed!
Name any evil beyond all evils—
that evil is the lot of Oedipus!

CHORUS OF THEBAN ELDERS
Whoever counseled you, counseled you wrong.
Far better had you died. Live blind, like this?

OEDIPUS
Advise me no more! What is done was done   1520
for the best! Only fools would not see that!
Could I have looked my father in the face
on finding him in Hades? Could I greet
my mother there, when even hanging me
will not atone for what I did to them?
Would I ever wish to see my children,
considering their corrupt conception?
These eyes could never have conceived of that!
Nor yet care to contemplate the city,
its wall, or the great statues of the gods   1530
and temples, from all of which I myself
myself had banned—I, who far more than most
delighted in the luxury of Thebes—
when my own lips pronounced that harsh command,
Let anyone who finds that man decried
by all the gods to be profane and fouled,
and descended from the stock of Laius,
expel and promptly purge him from his home!
And after I declared that it is I
who am defiled, could these two eyes confront   1540
unflinchingly the people's fearful stares?
Impossible! Could I have stopped the flow
of sound to my ears from morning till night,
I should have deafened myself, just like that!
so as to shut away this wretched self.

To live alone with one's thoughts, free at last
of sorrow's grip—what true joy that might be!
　　Ah, Cithaeron, why did you welcome me?
Why not seize and kill me, just where I stood,
and keep my birth a secret from all men?　　　　　　　　1550
O Polybus! O Corinth, ancient land!
Country that I once called my fathers' home,
what gorgeous colors you displayed, and all
to mask my hidden, festering disease!
My evil is exposed: I stand revealed:
I am the child of evil ancestors!
O, you three roads, your glade in the forest,
your thicket and faint path where three ways meet,
ways that drank my blood, drank my father's blood,
drank blood from these hands—have you so forgot　　　　1560
what I did there, and what I did when I
came here to Thebes? Marriage, marriage! Marriage
that gave me birth, that brought the same seed up,
and paraded fathers who were brothers,
children of incest who bloomed and grew ripe,
brides who mothered and married their husbands—
atrocious acts, abominable acts!
　　　To speak so hatefully of hateful things
is hateful in itself. Take me away,
and hide me somewhere in some foreign place;　　　　　1570
or kill me now, I beg of you; or else
throw me into the sea where you will not
be forced to look at me! Come, touch that man?
Come here! You won't touch him? Don't, I say!
No need to fear! Who else
can carry the weight of my woes but me?!
(Enter Creon with attendants.)

CHORUS OF THEBAN ELDERS
　　The only one left to assume your place
　　as guardian of this land is Creon.
　　He is here now. He'll answer to your needs.

OEDIPUS

    Creon! And what can I demand of him!   1580
    Why should he regard whatever I say?
    He knows I have done him nothing but wrong.

CREON

    Oedipus, of all the wrongs you did to me
    are past and gone. And I have not returned
    to revile or gloat at you.
(to attendants)
                      But, although
    you stand here shamelessly before us,
    please respect the holy fire of the Sun,
    which nourishes all things, and try to hide
    your infamy! The earth, the blessed rain,
    the light itself, can welcome you no more.   1590
    Take him, remove him instantly indoors!
    A kinsman's misfortune should not be seen
    except by kinsmen. His sorrows should not
    be known by all. Decency demands it.

OEDIPUS

    Let me ask you—since you have come to pay
    back good for evil, past whatever hope
    I might imagine would be possible—
    a favor . . . not for my sake, but for yours.

CREON

    What sort of favor could you have in mind?

OEDIPUS

    Expel me! As soon as you can! Send me   1600
    where no mortal creature will speak to me!

CREON

    For sure, you would have been removed by now—
    I needed first to hear it from the god
    himself, just what is to be done with you.

OEDIPUS

> That's been made altogether clear by him:
> allow this wicked parricide his death.

CREON

> So they said. Yet, given the way things work,
> it's better to be told what's best to do.

OEDIPUS

> Then you'll inquire about my wretched self?

CREON

> You'll not mock the words of the god this time!   1610

OEDIPUS

> No! And you'll do the proper thing, I trust:
> you shall yourself entomb your very own—
> that woman in the house. And don't force Thebes
> to keep me in my father's city here.
> And let me find my way to Cithaeron,
> that mountain which my parents meant to be
> my grave . . . and thus my death shall come to me
> from those who wished it for me when they lived.
>   One thing I know: nothing could have killed me;
> no sickness, no accident, no enemy—   1620
> I was preserved, and kept alive because
> some ghastly evil waited patiently.
> Let my fate lead me where it wishes to.
> When you come to consider my children,
> take no trouble for the boys. They're males;
> they'll find their legs and make their own way soon.
> Take pity on my two girls, though, for they
> were always with me: they sat at table
> and shared in everything. Care for them!
> And won't you let me touch them, and lament   1630
> my sorrows? Do, my lord! You're nobly born!

If I might place my hands on them, I could
imagine having them with me, as when
I once had eyes, and saw . . .
(Enter the daughters of Oedipus.)
                              What did I say?
Don't I hear my dear ones crying? Creon
has some pity for me, then? Am I right?
He sent to have my dearest ones brought here?

CREON

    I did. I knew the pleasures you had
    once enjoyed could—for a while—be yours.

OEDIPUS

    I wish you all the best, and may some god   1640
    lead you along the path better than I
    was led! Where are you, children? Come to me!
    Come to your brother's arms—these arms, whose hands
    did to your father's eyes, eyes once so bright,
    what had to be done: he who never saw,
    never knew that he was conceiving you
    in the woman from whom he too had come.
    I cannot see you, but I weep for you!
    Such bitterness you both will be dealt by life!
    Can there be banquets or celebrations   1650
    that might hold delights for you? Yes! And still,
    you shall return from them in sobs and tears!
    And when the time for marriage comes to you,
    what man alive would dare to face that risk,
    or accept the sneers and scorn your parents
    merited, but left you for your dowries?
    Shall any defamation go unsaid?
    Your father's father was killed by his son!
    Your father's mother made love with her son!
    And you're the offspring of that filthy one!   1660
    That's what you'll hear—so who would marry you?

No one, my dear children! Never! Ever!
Unmarried must you live, and barren die.
    And because we two who were their parents
now are dust and ash, son of Monoeceus,
the only father for these girls is you.
Don't look the other way while your nieces
wander the world unhusbanded like tramps;
don't let them fall into my pit of woes;
but feel for them, so young and so exposed,   1670
so helpless . . . should you fail to care for them.
You are noble: just nod your head and say
that you agree, just touch them with your hands!
Children, how many things could I tell you,
were you old enough to comprehend them,
and were there either time or place for us!
Since there is not, pray this for me instead:
that you may live, if life be granted you,
a better life than his that gave you life.

CREON

Tears; and tears; and tears. Get yourself inside!   1680

OEDIPUS

I'll do what I have to, like it or not.

CREON

What's done well's well done when its time has come.

OEDIPUS

Do you know the terms on which I will go?

CREON

You tell me. I'll know them when I've heard them.

OEDIPUS

You're to send me away from this country.

CREON
>   What you ask from me is the god's to give.

OEDIPUS
>   But the god loathes me!

CREON
>   That's why you'll get it!

OEDIPUS
>   Do you mean that?

CREON
>   Why should I waste my breath?

OEDIPUS
>   Take me away!

CREON
>   Let go of them! Clear out!

OEDIPUS
>   I will not have my children snatched from me!   1690

CREON
>   You're still presuming to do as you please?
>   Never in your life were you free to choose!
> *(Exit Oedipus, Creon, and attendants with the children.)*

CHORUS OF THEBAN ELDERS
>   People of Thebes! Consider Oedipus,
>   who was a man of might, and a great man
>   envied by our citizens for his luck,
>   all because the answer to that famous
>   riddle was his alone to give. And yet

a cruel storm blew up and he was wrecked.
So wait, and watch until the day is done.
Not one of us among the living here   1700
should be regarded fortunate unless
our death has come before we ever learn
just what it is to suffer human grief.

Oedipus at Colonus

Translated by
George Garrett

Closer to seventy than sixty, I rejoice in this old man's play. If memories and legends are true (and let us pray, in this case, that they are) Sophocles was in or about his nineties when he wrote *Oedipus at Colonus*. There's the story, one he could have dramatized himself, of how his family went to court to prove that the old man was senile or, anyway, incompetent to manage his own affairs; and the Court asked him what he was up to, what he was doing with himself and his life. And how Sophocles read to them some pages of this selfsame play. And how thereby he won the case, for better or worse.

There is always worse, isn't there, in the world of these tragedies? (Just as there is nothing, *nothing at all*, above and beyond laughter, hooting, and jeering in the great Greek comedies.) Some contemporary readers may remember, or at least have heard of, the sorrows of the poet Edwin Markham, whose family took him to court and proved his senility and incompetence on the witness stand. Years and years later, though also many years ago, I heard Robert Frost, at a small gathering, give a savagely funny imitation of the senile Markham on the stand. A moment later, even before the laughter of friends had died away, Frost, tears filling his eyes, said that he would have given anything, *anything*, to have written Markham's "The Man with a Hoe." Over the wasteland of centuries, Frost and Sophocles might well have understood each other, if not exactly each other's language.

Oedipus at Colonus is an old man's play. Though several generations are present on the stage—the young daughters; Polynices, the grown son; Theseus in his prime; hard-hearted Creon, calling himself old; likewise the Chorus, evidently of elders—it is riddled with the thoughts and feelings, the pains and fears and frustrations of the old. Having lived so long (and well, too, it seems, and at the perfect time, "the era of Athenian preeminence," Moses Hadas called it in his introduction for Jebb's *The Complete Plays of Sophocles*), Sophocles knew the story inside and out. Hadn't he danced, naked and glistening with oil, in the public celebrations for the defeat of the

Persians at Salamis? Even in ancient Greece not everyone had the figure and vigor and equipment for that. (There can't be half a dozen young poets, male or female, in our small planet who, out of the context of slapstick comedy, could grease up and dance nude for joy on [who knows?] the Fourth of July or VJ Day.) An exceptional youth followed by an incredible career during which he wrote more than a hundred plays, won many prizes and awards, held high public offices, and, what ought to be a great surprise for contemporary readers, was obviously well-liked, respected by his peers. Even Aristophanes treated him kindly. In all this he sounds a little like our Shakespeare, who also seems to have had precious few enemies.

For what we take, then, to be his final play, written in great old age and performed posthumously, a play centering on a suffering old man who, at the end, mysteriously transcends and overcomes his suffering and is allowed at last to rest in peace, Sophocles, while writing about what he knew well, turned again to the old myths (which he also knew by heart), to the story of Oedipus. It's a terrifying story, terrible to imagine, that is here retailed and rehearsed, and that comes, finally, to a quiet, calm closure. Getting there is not so quiet and calm. The old cliché, that most of the action in Greek tragedy takes place off-stage and comes to us through the Chorus as if reported by Jim Lehrer on *The News Hour*, is not quite the case. Plenty happens out of sight, especially the combat of Theseus and his Athenians against Creon and his Thebans, during which Theseus, truly heroic, rescues Antigone and Ismene and brings them safely back to their father. But plenty happens right on stage, too, including major confrontations and sometimes acts of violence—like Creon's people seizing Antigone and dragging her away. The confrontations, the life and death debates, are complex. Everybody, whether gripped by passion or tormented by desire, tries to be persuasive; they all try to present the best possible case for themselves, aiming, as it were, for the jury of the Chorus and, beyond them (the court of public opinion?). The audience of thousands, seated as if at a sports stadium, watch these huge, masked figures as they pose and move about, listening intently to what must have been splendidly projected shouts of poetry, not to mention singing and dancing. Some of the repetition and redundancy was surely required to be sure that basic points were made.

The people in the play, though their features are fixed in place on their masks, are constantly changing, revealing new and different aspects of themselves and their characters, as we see them interact with each other. Follow any one of them, Antigone, say, from faithful if weary caretaker, to thoughtful and persuasive daughter, to suicidal and grief-stricken child, to brave woman aiming, against the odds and maybe the Gods, to go home and try to prevent a slaughterhouse in Thebes. See how Polynices, at first impetuous and dishonorable, has, by the time of his farewell, earned some of your sympathy. Truth is, they are all electric with change. If this drama is—in form, not content—unsophisticated in our terms, pause to consider that almost all films, with their vast arsenal of technical controls and special effects, are unable to handle the difficulty and complexity of characters who can change without losing their essential core of being. Our best movies are lucky to maintain a simple consistency of character.

The one exception to the rule in this play, the most perfectly consistent being, is its one true hero—Theseus. Courage and honor are his strength and virtues. Both are tested more than once and in different ways. I believe you can learn a lot about the ideals of the Athenians, at the same time seeing that these are only ideals, perhaps only to be lived by and for an honest-to-God hero like Theseus. The rest of us, it goes without saying then and now, are usually running scared, full of sound and fury, promising anything to get what we think we want, and always rationalizing everything. The most we can hope for are celebrities, not heroes. Part of the tragedy of Oedipus is that he began as a hero and became a myth, a kind of celebrity. Here, by dying and dying well, he overcomes that burden and in popular memory (this play) becomes a powerful presence, a hero, again.

You would have to say, also, that Sophocles is offering a lifetime of wisdom to Athens. Here, at the peak of Athenian greatness, he celebrates the virtues which, in his view, made the city great—piety, honor, courage, hospitality, faith, tradition. And his celebration can be taken as a warning, too. Just so long as these virtues (and some others) prevail, just so long will Athens, or any great nation, prevail. That neither these virtues nor Athens managed to prevail (the Spartans defeated them two years after the death of Sophocles) gives a terrible edge to the tragedy, the sharp edge of historical irony which is where we are at home most of the time.

Finally, a word or two about translation and this translation. I have read a lot of them, prose and verse, and some very fine ones like the benchmark Fitts and Fitzgerald. In many ways one could not reasonably hope to improve on that one, any more than Fitts and Fitzgerald could not and did not imagine that they were doing "justice" to the original. But, as pretty much everybody agrees, they have done about as well as anyone ever has or ever will.

My goals were more modest and slightly different. If, as is undeniably the case, the words and works of Sophocles have remained magnificently the same, our own American language has been steadily changing itself, for better and for worse, in the past fifty years. And, a more complicated matter, the living, breathing, alive and kicking things *behind* the signs of our words, have changed also, perhaps more than any of us, who have lived in and through that half century and more, can realize. What am I saying? That I took liberties freely in the hope that I could translate some of the meaning for a reader in our curious culture where the existence of the word itself is often sorely threatened. That I obviously took liberties with the text while, at the same time, trying my best, as someone stuck in the late twentieth century, to be faithful to the original. Most likely more freedom, the liberty and license of adaptation would have served me and the great original (which, in any case, cannot be injured or improved by me or anyone else) better. But the game was not free and easy adaptation. It was, rather, somewhere in the vaguely defined precincts of translation. That my primary choice, the grounding of the whole, at the risk and expense of much that is beautiful and subtle, at the price that much of the poetry and nuance is inevitably not present, was for simplicity, a language that can at least be imagined (even nowadays) as being really spoken and heard by human beings and, sometimes, understood by them and us. I took as my guide and motto this sentence by Moses Hadas—"What is wanted and possible in a translation of Sophocles is not a reproduction of his art but the sense that the art is there."

What I am offering here at the outset is, then, a confession of one kind of failure, inexcusable perhaps, but, even so, not entirely without mitigation (I hope) and not without some sense of the terrible joys and sorrows of the old man's undying play.

OEDIPUS
ANTIGONE, daughter of Oedipus and Jocasta
MAN
CHORUS OF ELDERS
ISMENE, Antigone's sister
THESEUS, king of Athens
CREON, king of Thebes
POLYNICES, son of Oedipus
MESSENGER
NONSPEAKING
    Soldiers
    Guards

*(Near the grove of the Furies at Colonus, northwest of Athens.
    Oedipus enters, led by Antigone.)*

OEDIPUS
    Where are we now, my daughter?
    Tell me, if you can, Antigone, what place,
    what city this is. And tell me what stranger
    will make thank offerings on behalf
    of a poor blind beggar. I ask
    for next to nothing and I will take
    less than that as more than enough.

    Time has taught me the ways and means of pain.
    It is my honor and privilege to choose to be
    content. But tell me, daughter, my eyes,   10
    do you see some place nearby for me
    to rest myself on common ground
    or even a consecrated holy place?

Let me sit down here calmly and wait
for someone to tell us where we are.
We will listen and learn and then
we may have a thing or two to show and tell.

ANTIGONE

The city's walls and towers are miles away,
and this must be a sacred place. It is
a place of olive trees and laurel and of vines   20
where—hear them?—nightingales are singing.
Come here, old man, and rest easy on this rock.

OEDIPUS

Help me to sit down. Guard me, please.
I am only a helpless blind old man.

ANTIGONE

Whom I have been helping all this time.

OEDIPUS

Can you tell me where we are?

ANTIGONE

I don't know the name of this place,
but the city ahead is surely Athens.

OEDIPUS

Every traveler on the road
has told us that much.   30

ANTIGONE

Shall I go and find out
what this place is called?

OEDIPUS

Do that, child, go and see
if anyone lives around here.

ANTIGONE

There are people living nearby.
And I see a man not very far away.

OEDIPUS

Is he coming toward us?

ANTIGONE

He is coming here now. Speak to him.
Say whatever you have to say.
(Enter Man.)

OEDIPUS

Stranger, as you can clearly see,   40
my daughter's eyes must serve the two of us.
We would be most grateful if you would . . .

MAN

Before you talk any more you must
get up and leave this hallowed ground.

OEDIPUS

Hallowed to whom? What gods own this place?

MAN

It belongs to the Daughters of Earth
and Darkness. It is strictly forbidden
for you to be here.

OEDIPUS

To whom shall I be speaking, then,
when I make a prayer to them?   50

MAN

People around here call them
gentle and all-seeing goddesses.
And they have other names elsewhere.

OEDIPUS

> May they be gentle and forgiving,
> I pray; for I am here to stay.

MAN

> What are you saying?
> What do you mean?

OEDIPUS

> It was my fate to come and to be here.

MAN

> Then I must let you be until
> I can report this to the city.   60

OEDIPUS

> For God's sake, stranger, wait
> and hear me out. Please
> do not refuse to answer me.

MAN

> Ask what you will and I
> will not deny an answer.

OEDIPUS

> Tell me something more about this place.

MAN

> I will tell you all that I know.
> This whole place is sacred, belongs to Poseidon.
> Prometheus, the god of fire, is here
> also, and the place where you are is   70
> the doorway and bulwark of Athens.
> Those who live here say they are
> directly descended from Colonus, the great horseman.
> They take their name from him.
> True or false, that story lives in their hearts.

OEDIPUS

> Do they have a ruler
> or do they rule themselves?

MAN

> There is the king who lives in the city.

OEDIPUS

> And who is this powerful ruler?

MAN

> His name is Theseus. He is the son   80
> of the king called Aegeus.

OEDIPUS

> Can you deliver a message to him?

MAN

> What should I do that for?

OEDIPUS

> So that he can do me
> a small service in return
> for a very large reward.

MAN

> What does a wandering blind man
> have to offer a king?

OEDIPUS

> My words have bright eyes.

MAN

> Sir, judging by the look of you,   90
> you are a nobleman. For your sake
> I ask you to stay here
> while I go away to speak,

not to the people of the city,
but to those who live here,
who must decide among themselves
whether or not you can come and go.
(Exit Man.)

OEDIPUS

Has the stranger gone?

ANTIGONE

He has left us alone, father.
Say what you please in peace.   100

OEDIPUS

O dark gods, I pray, since I am
cast up upon your sacred shore, that you may be
merciful to me and to Apollo, who,
even as he foresaw the long years of evil
I must suffer, also swore that I will find
a home place and shelter among you,
and there shall earn an end to my bitter days,
bringing good fortune to all who receive me
and curses on those who try to drive me away.
Promised, likewise, there would be signs and portents,   110
earthquakes and terrible thunder and lightning.
I take it as a true sign that you have
somehow led me to this holy grove.
How else could I have ever wandered here
and found you first in a strange land,
a sober man among most sober gods?
How could I have even found this stone
to sit on unless it were a sign?
Dark goddesses, according to Apollo's word
vouchsafe to grant me now an end   120
to life unless I am beneath contempt,
a slave of suffering and pain. Hear me, I pray,

you daughters of darkness. Hear me, also, Athens,
most honored of all cities, city of Athena.
Have mercy now on Oedipus, a sad ghost,
a shadow of all the power and glory he once was.

ANTIGONE
Be quiet. Here come some elders
looking to find you.

OEDIPUS
I will be quiet. Hide me somewhere
near where I can listen to them   130
and choose a prudent course.
(Enter Chorus of elders.)

CHORUS
Where is he?
Who is he? What is his name?
Where has he gone,
this impudent stranger,
this man without shame?
Look for him.
Find him.
What man would dare
to violate this holy place   140
consecrated to the race
of gods we fear
to look at or
to listen for
or even to pray
to aloud?
Someone has come here
without reverence or fear.
Someone has come and dared
to ask for their blessing.   150
Where is he now?

OEDIPUS

> I am the man that you look for.
> I can see you with my listening ears.

CHORUS

> Oh, he is terrible
> to look at and terrible
> to hear . . .

OEDIPUS

> Please do not take me
> to be an outlaw.

CHORUS

> Lord, have mercy,
> who is this man?   160

OEDIPUS

> No one for you to envy,
> good defenders of this place.
> I am a man who must see
> through the eyes of another,
> who must cling like a child
> to this frail young girl.

CHORUS

> If you were blind
> from the day of your birth,
> then surely you have had
> a long life and a hard one.   170
> But, even so, we will
> not allow you to bring
> any judgment down upon us.
> Be careful, stranger,
> you have gone too far.
> Do not go any farther

into this place where silence is
the law and water runs
to mingle with pure honey.
Be careful. Come this way   180
and keep your distance.
If you have anything to say,
come away from forbidden ground
and speak where speech is allowed.

OEDIPUS
　　Daughter, what is the right thing
　　for us to do?

ANTIGONE
　　We must listen to them, father.
　　We should do what they say.

OEDIPUS
　　Give me your hand.

ANTIGONE
　　Here, I am holding on to you.   190

OEDIPUS
　　Strangers, can I trust you?
　　I ask you to be just.

CHORUS
　　No one will ever drive you
　　away from this place, old man.

OEDIPUS
　　Should I come closer?

CHORUS
　　Closer.

OEDIPUS
　　Closer?

CHORUS
> Lead him a little closer to us, girl.
> You can see how far to go.

ANTIGONE
> Follow me, father, follow   200
> with your blind steps
> behind me.

OEDIPUS
> I stumble along with baby steps.

ANTIGONE
> Be patient. Soon we'll be
> safe again on level ground.

OEDIPUS
> No one alive is safe for long.

CHORUS
> Stranger from a foreign land,
> learn to be brave.
> Learn to hate what the city hates.
> Study to honor what we hold dear.   210

OEDIPUS
> Let us do what we have to,
> daughter. Lead me to where
> we can speak and we can listen
> with some piety and respect.

CHORUS
> Be careful. Stop
> on the rock where you are.

OEDIPUS
> Here?

CHORUS
> Close enough.

OEDIPUS
> Shall I sit here?

CHORUS
> Yes. But move to the side a little.   220
> Sit on the edge of the rock.

ANTIGONE
> This is for me to do.
> Follow me, father, step by step.
> Lean yourself against my arm.

OEDIPUS
> I hate being blind!

CHORUS
> Tell us who you are,
> poor man, who suffer
> such pain and sorrow, what
> is your country called?

OEDIPUS
> I am a man who is in exile.   230
> Beyond that do not ask for more.

CHORUS
> Why not?

OEDIPUS
> My story is unspeakable.

CHORUS
> Tell us.

OEDIPUS
>   Daughter, what will become
>   of me now?

CHORUS
>   You have arrived at the raw edge
>   of the world. Speak openly to us.

OEDIPUS
>   Since there is no way I can hide
>   things from you, I will speak.   240

CHORUS
>   You have held back long enough.
>   Speak to us!

OEDIPUS
>   Have you ever heard
>   of the son of Laius?

CHORUS
>   God, have mercy on us.

OEDIPUS
>   And of the Labdacidae?

CHORUS
>   God, have mercy on us.

OEDIPUS
>   And of all the sorrows of Oedipus?

CHORUS
>   Are you that cursed man?

OEDIPUS
>   There is nothing I have to say   250
>   to you that you need to fear.

CHORUS
Horrible!

OEDIPUS
I am, indeed, cursed
and utterly miserable.

CHORUS
Horrible!

OEDIPUS
What will happen to us now, my daughter?

CHORUS
Go! Go! Get out of our country!

OEDIPUS
What became of all
your brave promises to me?

CHORUS
The man who lives to add   260
the sum of all his scars
and give the lie to liars
will choke upon his tears.
Leave this place here and now
for another place far away.
We do not need your share
of woe to fall on our lives.

ANTIGONE
I plead with you, righteous men,
if you cannot pity my father,
knowing the truth of what he's done,   270
then have mercy, please, on me
as I stand here speaking for him
and looking into your eyes

on behalf of him who has none.
Take me as one of your own, a child,
who prays compassion for an old man,
by all the things that are dear to you,
your women and children, your country and gods.
No matter how far you seek and look
you will never see any man escape his fate.   280

CHORUS
We pity you, daughter
of Oedipus.
We pity you both
for your sad fate.
But we also fear
what may come to us
from the hands of the gods.

OEDIPUS
What is the value of your good name?
What good is any kind of honor?
Athens has the reputation for   290
the grace of the gods and the earned right
to defend and protect any exile.
If this is true, then why do you
want to drive me away from here?
Is it all out of fear of my name?
For I have neither strength nor power
to harm you. All that I have done
is suffer myself. You fear me because
of the terrible story of my father and mother.
How can I be called evil,   300
who paid back once in kind
for a wrong done to me
without any knowledge or thought
and went on my way in ignorance
while those who ruined me knew
very well?

Thus in the name of the gods,
in all their honor and glory,
I beg you, strangers, to preserve
and protect me. The gods look down   310
upon the just and the unjust
and every mortal will be judged.
Do not tarnish the honor of Athens
with unholy and unjust actions,
but keep your promise to me
safe and sound. Though my face
is terrible to look at, still
I stand in the grace of the gods.
I can bring good things to this people.
And when your leader arrives,   320
he will hear and know everything.
Meantime I ask you to act with simple justice.

CHORUS

Old man, we hear and honor your thoughts
and the words that you have spoken.
Let our ruler decide this case.

OEDIPUS

And where is your ruler now?

CHORUS

In the city of our fathers.
The messenger who summoned us
has gone to bring him here.

OEDIPUS

Do you really think he will come   330
this far for the sake of one blind man?

CHORUS

As soon as he hears your name,
he will come here at once.

OEDIPUS

> How will he know my name?

CHORUS

> News comes from the mouths of travelers
> even on the longest road.
> You can be sure he will come.
> Old man, your name is known
> all over the world, and even if
> he's resting, he will rise and come.   340

OEDIPUS

> Good luck to this city
> and to myself as well.
> What honorable man does not
> hold himself in honor?

ANTIGONE

> My God, father, what shall I say?
> What can I think?

OEDIPUS

> What is the matter,
> Antigone, my child?

ANTIGONE

> I can see a woman
> coming toward us   350
> riding a Sicilian colt.
> She's wearing a Thessalian
> hat that hides her face.
> What can I say?
> Is she or is she not?
> My mind is wandering
> and I can't be sure.
> Oh, to be sure, it is

nobody else but she,
and she smiles a greeting.   360
It is my sister Ismene.

OEDIPUS

What are you saying?

ANTIGONE

I can see her, your daughter,
my sister, she's here,
and you shall know her
by her familiar voice.
(Enter Ismene.)

OEDIPUS

Have you truly come to us, child?

ISMENE

Father, I grieve to see
what has become of you.

OEDIPUS

Are you really and truly here?   370

ISMENE

It was not easy for me.

OEDIPUS

Touch me, daughter.

ISMENE

I will reach for you both.

OEDIPUS

Oh, sisters, my children!

ISMENE

A portrait of misery.

OEDIPUS

Do you mean my unhappiness and hers?

ISMENE

And my own.

OEDIPUS

Why are you here?

ISMENE

I was sick with worrying over you.

OEDIPUS

Did you long to see me?   380

ISMENE

Yes. And I have brought some news.
I came with my one faithful servant
to bring you this news.

OEDIPUS

Your brothers should be here, too.
Why aren't they? Where are they now?

ISMENE

They are wherever they may be.
It is a very hard time for them.

OEDIPUS

They are acting like Egyptians,
where the men stay home to work
over the stove and the loom   390

while their women go forth to earn
a living. Just so, daughters,
those who ought to be here are at home
like spoiled girls while you two bear
the burden of your father's sorrows.
This one has wandered with me
ever since her childhood, leading
the way, barefoot in the wilderness,
all too often racked by hunger,
soaked by rain and burned 400
by the sun, suffering these things
so that her father might be kept alive.
And you, too, my child, came once
before, secretly, to tell me
what the prophecies about me are.
You have always been faithful to me.
And now what do you have to tell me,
Ismene? What has brought you here?
You haven't come without some good reason.
Is there something I should be afraid of? 410

ISMENE
Because I do not wish to suffer
the same pains twice, I will not
rehearse the story of my own troubles,
the hard times I've endured to find you.
I am here to report on the evils
that have befallen your unlucky sons.
At first they agreed that Creon should have
the throne, and thus the city could be free
of its curse from our suffering family.
But then, thanks to a dark God 420
and to the curse created by us,
they both began to lust for royal power.
The younger brother deprived his senior,
Polynices, of the kingship

and banished him from the land.
Rumor has it that he lives
in exile in the valleys of Argos,
and that he has married and gathered
together a band of friends and allies,
planning to capture Thebes or die.   450
The rumors are more than idle words.
They are true. And as for yourself,
I cannot discover when and if
the gods will take pity on you.

OEDIPUS

Is there any hope
the gods will notice me
some day and save me?

ISMENE

The latest prophecies
seem to be saying so.

OEDIPUS

How do they say so?   460
What do the oracles say?

ISMENE

They say that the time will come,
before your death and afterward,
when the people will turn to you for help.

OEDIPUS

What can they possibly gain
from someone like myself?

ISMENE

They will come to look to you
for power and protection.

OEDIPUS

> But how can that be when I
> have no strength or power left?   470

ISMENE

> The gods who ruined your life
> will choose to raise you up again.

OEDIPUS

> What kind of blessing is this—
> to lift up an old man who fell
> down in the prime of his life?

ISMENE

> It is because of all this
> that Creon will come to you,
> and he will be coming soon.

OEDIPUS

> For what purpose?
> Tell me, my daughter.   480

ISMENE

> They will move you close to Thebes,
> there where you can be near,
> but may not enter the land.

OEDIPUS

> But what do they gain if I
> am not even in the city?

ISMENE

> The place of your tomb
> could cause them great harm.

OEDIPUS

> Even without a God's inspiration
> a man might guess that much.

ISMENE
> And that is exactly why   490
> they need mastery over you.

OEDIPUS
> Will they bury me in Theban earth?

ISMENE
> That is not allowed
> because you killed your father.

OEDIPUS
> Then they will never master me.

ISMENE
> That will be a heavy burden
> on the hearts of our people.

OEDIPUS
> How can that be, my child?

ISMENE
> They will feel the terrible anger,
> the rage coming from your tomb.   500

OEDIPUS
> How did you learn these things?

ISMENE
> From envoys who came back from Delphi.

OEDIPUS
> And all these things were truly
> spoken about me?

ISMENE
> According to the men
> who returned to Thebes.

OEDIPUS
>Have either of my sons heard this?

ISMENE
>Both of them know all about it.

OEDIPUS
>And yet those scoundrels care
>more for the throne than me.   510

ISMENE
>It wounds me to say it,
>but we must endure the truth.

OEDIPUS
>May the gods preserve their fiery rage,
>and let me be the final judge between them
>as they raise their spears in fratricidal war.
>He who holds the throne will surely lose it
>and he who is in exile is gone for good.
>When I was banished, neither one
>of them came forth to my aid to defend me.
>They turned away and permitted me to be   520
>proclaimed an exile and driven from home.
>Some may well say that was my secret wish.
>But that's not true. On that same day,
>when I was still on fire with passion,
>I begged to be stoned to death,
>but not one stepped forward to do it.
>After a time, when my pain had eased,
>just as I began to understand my hatred
>of myself was much too much to bear,
>then the city acted, forced me   530
>to leave them behind, to go away.
>My sons might have saved me, but refused.
>They did not speak a word in my behalf.
>And these two here, these two young girls,

alone have fed and sheltered and led me,
while their heartless ungrateful brothers
were each scheming to become the king.
I will not become the ally of either,
and they will gain nothing at all,
I am sure, from all the prophecies   540
brought by Ismene and to be fulfilled at last.
Then let them send Creon to seek me out,
or anyone else of power and influence;
for if you strangers, who preserve this place
with the help of the gods, will give me protection,
then you will gain a staunch defender
and will cause much trouble for my enemies.

CHORUS

You and your daughters have earned our pity,
and now that you offer to be a protector
of this place, I can give you some good advice.   550

OEDIPUS

Speak and I'll do what you ask.

CHORUS

First of all, you must purify this place
in the name of the gods on whose earth you stood.

OEDIPUS

How can I do that, strangers?
Tell me.

CHORUS

Clean and purify your hands.
Then bring libations from the sacred springs.

OEDIPUS

And what shall I do next?

CHORUS
>There are basins, made by a gifted artist.
>Crown them on top and at the handles.   560

OEDIPUS
>With what?
>Branches or woolen cloth?

CHORUS
>With the new fleece
>of a young lamb.

OEDIPUS
>And how should I perform the rite?

CHORUS
>Face the morning sun and pour.

OEDIPUS
>Do I pour from the bowls you spoke of?

CHORUS
>In three streams,
>and empty the last one.

OEDIPUS
>Tell me how it should be filled.   570

CHORUS
>With water and honey,
>but add no wine.

OEDIPUS
>And after the leafstrewn earth
>receives this libation?

CHORUS

> Then lay down three times nine
> of olive twigs and say the prayers.

OEDIPUS

> This is important. I need to hear it.

CHORUS

> Because they are called the Kindly Ones,
> pray they may receive and protect you
> with kindly hearts. The suppliant   580
> should ask this in a soft voice,
> then leave at once without looking back.
> If you do these things, then I
> will stand by you firmly, but if not,
> then I fear for you, stranger.

OEDIPUS

> Daughters, have you heard
> the people of this place?

ISMENE

> We have heard them.
> Tell us what you want us to do.

OEDIPUS

> Since I am weak and blind, I need   590
> one of you to perform these rites.
> One person, alone, can make a sacrifice for many
> if it is all done with deep sincerity.
> Go quickly. But do not leave me here.
> I can't move without a guiding hand.

ISMENE

> I'll go now to perform the rite.
> But where, exactly, should I go?

CHORUS
> Go to the other side of these woods.
> There's a man who will help you if you need it.

ISMENE
> You stay here, Antigone.   600
> Look after our father.
> It is no great burden
> to care for a father.

(Exit Ismene.)

CHORUS
> Stranger, it is a fearful thing
> to waken old evils from deep sleep.
> Yet we must have the truth from you.

OEDIPUS
> What are you saying?
> What is it you are asking for?

CHORUS
> Speak to us here and now   610
> about the awful pain and sorrow
> you have been suffering.

OEDIPUS
> For the sake and customs
> of hospitality, permit me,
> please, the privilege of silence.

CHORUS
> People tell versions of your story everywhere.
> But we want to hear the truth of it.

OEDIPUS
> Oh, God!

CHORUS
> Do what we ask, I beg you.

OEDIPUS
> Oh, the sorrow and the pity of it!

CHORUS
> Grant this request, stranger,   620
> and we shall grant yours.

OEDIPUS
> I have suffered and endured
> evils beyond believing,
> as God is my witness.
> But I did none of it by choice.

CHORUS
> Then how and for what?

OEDIPUS
> In perfect ignorance I was married
> in an evil union by my city.

CHORUS
> Who was it shared your infamous bed?
> Was it, as they tell it, your own mother?   630

OEDIPUS
> It is a kind of death
> to have to say this,
> but these two girls, my daughters . . .

CHORUS
> What are you saying?

OEDIPUS
> That these two are the fruit
> of my mother's womb.

CHORUS
> Then they are more than daughters.

OEDIPUS
> They are also my own sisters.

CHORUS
> Surely you have suffered greatly.

OEDIPUS
> What I have suffered is far beyond   640
> the powers of your imagination
> and beyond my power to forget.

CHORUS
> And you have sinned greatly.

OEDIPUS
> No. I have not sinned.

CHORUS
> How can you dare to say that?

OEDIPUS
> Can't you see? It was my reward
> for service to the state.
> I should never have done that service.

CHORUS
> And then, stranger, isn't it true
> that you also committed murder?   650

OEDIPUS
> What are you asking?
> What do you want to know?

CHORUS
> Did you murder your own father?

OEDIPUS

> You wound me again and again.
> Pain upon pain upon pain . . .

CHORUS

> There is no acceptable explanation.

OEDIPUS

> There is a plea that I can make.
> I was in the grip of rage.
> And, according to the law, I'm not
> guilty. I acted in madness and ignorance.   660

CHORUS

> Look, blind man, here comes our king,
> Theseus, son of Aegeus,
> summoned here as you wanted.
> (*Enter Theseus.*)

THESEUS

> I've heard your story many times,
> son of Laius, how you put out your own eyes.
> And now I see you as you really are.
> Your clothing and your wounded face
> tell all the world your dreadful name.
> I offer my pity, but I must know
> what it is you want from me and the city.   670
> You and your companion must tell me.
> It will have to be something terrible
> beyond believing for me to deny you.
> Always remember I was an exile, too.
> I, too, struggled against incredible dangers.
> And I would never turn away
> from aid and comfort to another like myself.
> I, too, am only a man
> who has no more share and hope
> for the future than you do.   680

OEDIPUS

    Theseus, your words and your nobility
    leave me with only a little to say.
    All that remains is for me to tell
    what it is I am asking from you.

THESEUS

    Then tell me. What do you want?

OEDIPUS

    I want to offer you a gift.
    I offer myself in all my ugliness
    with a promise of good things to come.

THESEUS

    What good things do you promise?

OEDIPUS

    You will learn that all in good time.   690

THESEUS

    And when will these things be known?

OEDIPUS

    When I am dead and when you bury me.

THESEUS

    Your request concerns only final things.
    Have you forgotten you must live until then?
    Or do you think of your life as nothing?

OEDIPUS

    It all has to do with my burial.

THESEUS

    This is no great favor to ask of me.

OEDIPUS

Be careful.
It is not so simple as it seems.

THESEUS

Do you expect troubles from your sons?   700

OEDIPUS

They will try to take me back.

THESEUS

Then why not go home with them?
It is not proper to remain in exile.

OEDIPUS

I was not allowed to live there
when I wanted to and needed to.

THESEUS

There is no value in anger
when you are in deep trouble.

OEDIPUS

Spare me your rebukes,
at least until I've finished.

THESEUS

If I am ignorant, teach me the truth.   710

OEDIPUS

Theseus, I have been wounded many times.

THESEUS

Are you talking about your family curse?

OEDIPUS

Every Greek knows that story by heart.

THESEUS
>   Then what is this unbearable affliction
>   that is more than you can bear?

OEDIPUS
>   Picture it as it is.
>   I was exiled from my country
>   by my own sons and now
>   I can never return there
>   because I killed my father.   720

THESEUS
>   Then how can they bring you back?

OEDIPUS
>   The oracle has told them to do so.

THESEUS
>   And what is the fate they bear?

OEDIPUS
>   They fear they'll be killed in this country.

THESEUS
>   How on earth could that come to pass?

OEDIPUS
>   Ah, son of Aegeus, only the gods
>   never know old age, never know death.
>   Everything else is drowned in time.
>   Like the body, the strength of nations
>   weakens, fades, and disappears.   730
>   Loyalty turns into treachery,
>   and, as the spirit among friends
>   is forever changing, so also with kingdoms
>   where good times lead to bitter.
>   And then again friendship blooms.

If the sun shines on you and Thebes,
time will soon enough bring dark clouds,
and spears will shatter your treaties and pledges.
And if Zeus is still himself and if his son,
Phoebus, still tells truth, then my body,   740
dead and buried and cold, will drink
warm blood . . .
Still, there is no good or pleasure
in telling things that ought to be secret.
Honor your promise, keep your word,
and you will never have to say
that Oedipus, whom you welcomed,
was unworthy of hospitality.
Unless, of course, the gods have lied to me.

CHORUS

My Lord, from the outset it has been   750
clear that this stranger keeps his word.

THESEUS

Who dares to turn away from his good will?
First, according to natural law, he is
entitled to enjoy an ally's hearth.
And he has come here as a suppliant
of our gods and promises to pay
honorable rewards to our country and me.
I respect these things and will not reject
his kindness ever. I therefore declare
him to be a citizen of our country.   760
If it pleases him to stay here,
I appoint you to be his guards.
Or, if he chooses, he can come with me.
Oedipus, I offer you the choice.

OEDIPUS

May the gods bless you with great good fortune.

THESEUS

What do you want to do?
Will you come with me to the palace?

OEDIPUS

I would gladly come with you,
but here is the right place for me.

THESEUS

The right place for what?   770
Speak. I'm not against you.

OEDIPUS

Here is the place where I will overcome my enemies.

THESEUS

Your presence is a powerful blessing.

OEDIPUS

Only if you honor the pledge you made.

THESEUS

Count on it. I shall never break faith.

OEDIPUS

And I will never demand an oath from you.

THESEUS

All that you can have or need is my word.

OEDIPUS

And what will you do?

THESEUS

What is it that you are afraid of?

OEDIPUS
That men will come against me.   780

THESEUS
These men here will see to them.

OEDIPUS
But when you leave me here . . .

THESEUS
Don't try to teach me what to do.

OEDIPUS
My heart is heavy with the weight of fear.

THESEUS
You can be sure I feel nothing like that.

OEDIPUS
Because you do not know the danger.

THESEUS
No man will try to take you away
from here against my will. Their threats
and furious words are without meaning
and they know it, too. If these men   790
have bragged that they will seize you,
consider that the sea they must cross
is wide and rough going. I urge you,
sir, to be of stout heart. Quite aside
from my pledge and my firm decision,
if it truly was Apollo who guided you here,
you are perfectly safe. My name is your bodyguard.
(*Exit Theseus.*)

CHORUS
> Here is a home for fine horses,
> stranger, white Colonus where
> the furtive nightingale hides and sings   800
> and vines and flowers scent the air.
>
> Here is a place untroubled by
> the heat of the sun, winds of the cold.
> Here Dionysus comes and goes
> in every season, green and gold.
>
> Here the dew from heaven falls
> to feed the flowers of the gods.
> Where crocus and narcissus call
> out holy names, we kneel to pray.
>
> From here the river rises up   810
> to flow across the fertile plain.
> Here the Muses form a choir
> and Aphrodite smiles again.
>
> And our fair land has something rare
> that I am told grows nowhere
> else beneath the sun—an olive tree
> that cannot die, cannot be killed.
>
> And last we raise our voice in praise
> of Athens, best gift of the gods,
> shining city for all our days,   820
> home for mighty horses, dancing gods.
>
> Here Lord Poseidon chose to give
> us the tools and tricks to train
> our horses and gave us, too, the strength to live
> freely and wisely on land and sea.

ANTIGONE

> Your homeland is justly praised.
> But now is the test if words are true.

OEDIPUS

> What is happening now, my daughter?

ANTIGONE

> Creon himself is coming here,
> and he has many others with him.   830

OEDIPUS

> And now, kind friends, the time has come
> to prove you can protect me.

CHORUS

> Fear not, Oedipus, we may be
> old, but we shall prove our power.
> *(Enter Creon with guards.)*

CREON

> Gentlemen of Athens, I can read
> fear in your eyes without good cause.
> For I have come here to act in peace,
> and I know this city has great power,
> as much as any in all of Greece.
> But even so, and as old as I may be,   840
> I have come to bring this man back to Thebes,
> at the request of the Theban people
> and because I am his kith and kin.
> And you, poor suffering Oedipus,
> hear me here and now. The people
> call you home. I grieve for you.
> I feel your pain and the misery of exile,
> a wandering beggar with only one person
> to care for you, and she, poor girl,

has fallen far from her beauty and grace,   850
unmarried at her age and vulnerable.
This is the bitter truth of things, old man.
In the name of the gods and for the sake
of your family, I ask you to agree
to come back home, the home of your blood.
Bid farewell to friendly Athens
and once again show reverence for Thebes,
for it was Thebes that first raised you high.

OEDIPUS
You who are utterly without honesty,
who can turn even the plain truth into a lie,   860
why are you trying to do this?
Why are you setting a trap for me?
When I was sick unto death with grief,
when I would gladly have given up the ghost,
you refused to allow me my deepest wish.
Later when my rage and grief played out,
and my one hope was to live at home,
you drove me into exile, never even
considering the kinship you now talk of.
And so you find me in this place   870
where these good people look kindly on me.
And still you are scheming to take me away.
You say cruel things with soft, smooth words.
You take pleasure charming others to act
against their wills. Suppose that someone
gave you nothing when you were in desperate need,
that this man would not even offer sympathy;
and then, later on, when you needed nothing
from him, he suddenly offered everything
he had denied before, wouldn't that be   880
a vain and pointless pleasure?
And this is precisely what you offer now,
something well disguised in pleasing words.

I tell these good men the simple truth,
that you and your designs are evil.
You have come not to take me to my home
but instead to put me out of our city,
so that the city can escape my curse
and the troubles that will come from here.
But that will not happen. What will come to pass   890
is the terror of my vengeful ghost.
All the land my sons will ever own
is just enough space to die in.
Which of us knows the true fate of Thebes?
It is I who have listened to Apollo and to Zeus,
his holy father. You vomit your lies.
Your words can only hurt your case.
I know there is no way to persuade you,
so I ask you to leave us and go
away in peace. Let me live here,   900
and I shall be contented with my life.

CREON

Who do you think is wounded by your words?
You only manage to hurt yourself.

OEDIPUS

As long as you fail to convince me,
or these others, I can be happy.

CREON

The years, which should have brought wisdom,
have only earned you shame and discontent.

OEDIPUS

You are gifted with a quick, sharp tongue,
but no man is eloquent in every case.

CREON

I do not speak grandly. I tell truth.   910

OEDIPUS

> I see . . . and what you say
> is pithy and appropriate?

CREON

> Not appropriate for a mind like yours.

OEDIPUS

> Go! Leave us alone! I speak on behalf
> of all of us. Don't try to guard
> this place where I must live.

CREON

> I am speaking to them, not you.
> I ask all to bear witness to your words.
> And if I get my hands on you . . .

OEDIPUS

> Who would dare to touch me here?   920

CREON

> I promise that you will suffer great pain
> without so much as any touch by me.

OEDIPUS

> What does that strange threat mean?

CREON

> That I have already captured your daughter
> and sent her away. Soon I shall
> take away this other one.

OEDIPUS

> Oh, God . . . !

CREON

> Soon enough you'll be full of sorrow.

OEDIPUS
>You have taken my other daughter?

CREON
>And I will have this one, too.   930

CHORUS
>You must leave at once, stranger.
>You have proved yourself unworthy.

CREON
>Whether she's willing or not,
>take this girl away.

ANTIGONE
>Oh, God, to whom can I turn
>now in my hour of need?
>*(Guards seize Antigone.)*

CHORUS
>What are you doing, stranger?

CREON
>I will not lay hands on him,
>but she belongs to me.

CHORUS
>What you are doing is all wrong.   940

CREON
>No. It is just.

CHORUS
>How can that be?

CREON
>I am taking back what is already mine.

OEDIPUS

I call upon the city of Athens!

CHORUS

Think what you are doing, stranger,
and let the girl go. Must we
settle this matter with bloodshed?

CREON

Stand back!

CHORUS

I will not. This is a crime.

CREON

It will be war if you try to stop me.   950

OEDIPUS

See, it is exactly as I warned you.

CHORUS *(to guards)*

Let the girl go now.

CREON

Commands without power are empty.

CHORUS

I say again. Let her go.

CREON

And I repeat, get out of my way.

CHORUS

Men of Athens, we are being
attacked! Come quick! Come now!

ANTIGONE
>Help me, good people!
>They are dragging me away.

OEDIPUS *(groping)*
>Where are you, my daughter?   960

ANTIGONE
>Here. I am being taken away.

OEDIPUS
>Give me your hands, child.

ANTIGONE
>I am too weak.

CREON *(to guards)*
>Take her away from here.
>*(Guards drag Antigone out.)*

OEDIPUS
>O holy Gods, come help me now.

CREON
>Your two living crutches will never help you
>walk again. Since you hope to defeat
>your own country and your own people,
>then this is your victory. All in due time
>you'll learn that nothing you are doing   970
>or have ever done was right and just.
>Rage ruled you and has been your ruin.

CHORUS *(to Creon)*
>Halt, stranger, where you are.

CREON
>Don't touch me, I tell you.

CHORUS
>   I won't let go.
>   You have stolen the two.

CREON
>   It will cost you more than the two girls.

CHORUS
>   What are you saying?

CREON
>   I'll take the old man and carry him away.

CHORUS
>   That's a mad and foolish thing to say.   980

CREON
>   And I will do it, too, unless
>   your king is able to stop me.

OEDIPUS
>   Voice without shame,
>   will you dare to touch me?

CREON
>   I tell you to keep quiet.

OEDIPUS
>   Let the goddesses of this place
>   allow me to lay a curse on you,
>   you who have blinded the one bright eye
>   of my life, like the seeing eyes I lost long ago.
>   May the blessed sun which sees everything   990
>   see to it you have an old age like mine.

CREON
>   Athenians, you are witness to his words.

OEDIPUS
They can clearly see us both.
They see my sole defense is words.

CREON
This is more than I will endure.
I may be an old man and alone,
but I'll carry this creature away with me.

CHORUS
That is unforgivable arrogance.
Don't even think about it.

CREON
I think I'll do it here and now.   1000

CHORUS
Not while our city is alive.

CREON
Given just cause, a man can overcome
any foe.

OEDIPUS
Listen to what he is saying.

CHORUS
As God is my witness, he shall not succeed.

CREON
God knows the whole truth.
You do not.

CHORUS
Stranger, this is a criminal act.

CREON

> Crime or not, you have no choice
> but to endure it.   1010

CHORUS

> I call upon our people. I call
> our captains to come and defend us.
> *(Enter Theseus, accompanied by soldiers.)*

THESEUS

> What's going on? What has happened
> to make you cry for help and interrupt
> the sacrifice to the God of the sea,
> our blessed protector? Tell me why
> I had to come running to be with you.

OEDIPUS

> My friend, I know you by your voice.
> This man has done a terrible thing.

THESEUS

> Who is this person? Tell me about it.   1020

OEDIPUS

> This is Creon, who has captured
> and carried off my daughters.

THESEUS

> What is it you are telling me?

OEDIPUS

> It is just as I have said.

THESEUS *(to his soldiers)*

> First, one of you go running
> to the altars and order the people

to cease and desist with the sacrifice,
and to hurry, on foot and horseback,
to the place where the highways join.
These captive girls must not pass that place   1030
or this man will make a fool of me.
Go now and do these things.

(Exit soldier.)

Now, as for this person, if I should treat him as he deserves
he would already be bloody from wounds.
But he will be tried and tested
according to the laws and customs
of his own place and people.

(to Creon)

Believe me, you will never leave
this country until you have brought the girls
back and set them free in front of me.   1040
What you have done is a disgrace to me
and a cause of shame for you and your country.
You have come to a city that lives by law
and honors justice. And you have broken
our law, ignoring the admonitions of authority
as if you could do what you please by force.
You believed my city had no brave men
and that I was king of nothing at all.
Surely you didn't learn this in Thebes.
Thebes is not a breeding place for criminals,   1050
and they would not praise you if they learned
you were robbing me and insulting the holy gods
by making hostages of our suppliants.
I would never come into your land,
even on behalf of a just cause,
without permission of your ruler,
whoever he might be. I would know
how a stranger is supposed to act and behave
among the good citizens of your city.

CREON

    I never said your city has no good men,   1060
    son of Aegeus, and neither was it rash
    for me to act as I have done.
    I never imagined that your people
    would keep my kinfolk here against their will.
    I could not believe that they would welcome
    a polluted creature who killed his father,
    one whose children are the incestuous
    offspring of his own mother.
    I knew well the wisdom of the Areopagus,
    and I sincerely believed that Athens   1070
    would not be a home for wanderers
    like these. I took him to be lawful prey.
    Still, I would never have tried to touch him
    if he hadn't cursed my family and me.
    I took it as my lawful right to pay
    back injuries and insults in kind.
    You know that anger is ageless.
    Only the dead are free from it.
    Do, then, as you will. My cause
    is wholly just. Though I am old and alone,   1080
    bear in mind that I will hold
    you responsible for all that you do.

OEDIPUS

    O arrogance without a shred or scent of shame!
    Do you insult my old age and yours
    with all this talking of murders and marriages,
    or curses and disasters? I suffered all
    these things in ignorance and innocence
    to please the gods, who certainly must hate
    our family. What fault have you found
    in me that made me do these things?   1090
    And tell me this: if my father had heard

from the oracle that he would die
at the hands of his children, how can you
blame me for that? I was not born
or even conceived. And when I came
into being and one day killed my father
in a fight, completely ignorant of who he was,
how can you justly blame me for that?
And aren't you ashamed of speaking about
my marriage to my mother, who was,   1100
after all, your sister? Now I will
speak of it myself, since you have opened
the subject with your unholy mouth.
Yes, she carried me and gave birth
to me, but neither of us knew the truth.
And she also bore my children, to my shame.
This much is certain. You slander us both
on purpose, whereas I would never have married her
if I had known, nor would I speak of it.
Nothing, not that marriage, not the murder   1110
of my father, both of which you curse me for,
will ever prove that I am evil.
Answer me this one question, if you can.
If you were attacked by a perfect stranger,
would you ask him if he is your father?
Or would you fight back to save your life?
These sorrows come to me from the gods.
If my father's ghost had life and breath,
he would say the same thing now.
You, though, out of your essential wickedness,   1120
can say anything you please, even the unspeakable,
and rebuke me in the presence of these people.
You will flatter Theseus face to face
and praise the ways and means of Athens.
But you have forgotten one great truth—
that of all the nations this one knows
best how to serve and honor the gods.

And yet you come here to seize me,
a helpless old man and a suppliant.
And you have kidnaped my daughters.   1130
For these things, I do beseech the goddesses
of this holy place to hear and to answer
my prayers. May you soon learn
the nature of the men who guard this city.

CHORUS

Lord, this man is worthy and just
and he deserves our aid and comfort.

THESEUS

We have talked long enough.
While we are talking, the criminals are escaping.

CREON

Tell me what I must do.

THESEUS

Show me the way, and there will be   1140
no other guardian but myself alone.
I know very well you would never have done
the things that you've done without
armed men with you at your service
to give you the confidence to act.
Take me and show me where you are holding
the two girls captive. And if your people
have carried them out of this country
there are those who will follow them
and none of you will live to thank the gods.   1150
Come now, lead on. And bear in mind
the captor is now captive, the hunter is caught
in his own trap. What you have taken
by trickery will now be taken back.
Do you understand the truth of this,
or have our words been wholly wasted?

CREON
> While we are here your word is law,
> but in my country my will is done.

THESEUS
> Make threats if you want to, but go now.
> And you, Oedipus, stay here in peace.   1160
> You have my promise that, unless I die,
> I will deliver your daughters safely to you.

OEDIPUS
> Blessings on you, Theseus, your heart
> is noble and what you do is just.
> *(Exeunt Theseus, Creon, and attendants.)*

CHORUS
> How I wish that I could be
> there where the enemy will stand and fight,
> close by the place, dear to Apollo,
> or on the torchlit shore where holy rites
> are performed by Eleusinian priests.

> There Theseus, the warrior, will fight   1170
> to free the virgin sisters from
> captivity. And then the city will rejoice
> and thank our gods with grateful voice.

> Now they must be coming near
> the western mountains, fleeing home
> on horses or in chariots of fear.
> For every one of them will fall.

> The gods are with us, one and all.
> Our fearless horsemen, who have never known
> defeat, will give their lives if need be   1180
> to save the honor of Athens.

Are they fighting yet or not?
I can hear voices in my mind,
a prophecy that tells me soon
the daughters of Oedipus will be
free again and free from suffering.
God has a plan and purpose for
this day. We shall have a victory.

Lord of the gods, all-seeing Zeus,
vouchsafe that victory to our city.   1190
Athena, Apollo, Daphne, too,
give us good aid and comfort now.

Old man, wanderer, we have told
the truth and guarded you without fear.
Now we can see them coming here,
your daughters and our warriors.

OEDIPUS

Where are they?
What are you saying?
(Enter Antigone, Ismene, Theseus, and soldiers.)

ANTIGONE

Father, oh, my father,
if only the gods would let you see   1200
the noble man who has rescued us.

OEDIPUS

Are both of you here, my child?

ANTIGONE

Theseus and his men have saved us.

OEDIPUS

Come nearer, daughter, let me embrace
you who I feared were lost for good.

ANTIGONE
>What you ask is what we long for.

OEDIPUS
>But where are you?

ANTIGONE
>We are coming nearer to you.

OEDIPUS
>My dearest daughters . . .

ANTIGONE
>All children are dear to loving parents.   1210

OEDIPUS
>You two are the crutches that carry me.

ANTIGONE
>Sad crutches for a sorrowful man.

OEDIPUS
>Now that I have and hold what is most dear
>to me, I am not afraid to die.
>Hold me close and tight and tell me
>in a few words how it was.

ANTIGONE
>Here is the man who saved us,
>father. Listen to what he says.

OEDIPUS
>Forgive me, friend, for speaking first
>to my daughters who've come back to me.   1220
>I am beholden to you for all this joy.
>It is you, and you alone, who saved them.

May the gods grant all my best wishes
for you and your fair country,
where I have found true piety
and justice and words without lies.
Give me your hand, good king.
Permit me to kiss your cheeks.
But what am I saying?
How can I ask you to touch   1230
someone like myself, a man
polluted by many evil things?
I cannot, will not ask you this,
nor to try to imagine my misery.
Accept my salutation where you are.
Be for me what you have justly been.

THESEUS

It is fitting and proper for you to talk
first at length with your daughters
and not with me. Let my actions
speak for themselves as no words can.   1240
Consider that I have kept the promises
I made to you, and here I am
bringing these girls, alive and unhurt
in spite of all the threats against them.
As for the fight, let them tell you.
But share your wisdom with me
about a surprising thing that has happened,
something that may be inconsequential, or may not.

OEDIPUS

What is it, son of Aegeus?
Tell me what I need to know.   1250

THESEUS

They say that a man has come here,
not from Thebes, but nevertheless

calling himself your kinsman.
He is now sitting at the altar of Poseidon,
the place where I was making sacrifice.

OEDIPUS

Where has he come from?
What is the purpose of his prayers?

THESEUS

I only know he wants to speak to you
on a matter of no great importance.

OEDIPUS

But if he is a suppliant, if he is   1260
at prayer, it must be serious.

THESEUS

They say he wants to speak to you
and then return the way he came.

OEDIPUS

Who can the man at the altar be?

THESEUS

Do you have any kinsmen in Argos
who might want to ask a favor of you?

OEDIPUS

Don't say any more, my friend.

THESEUS

What's the matter?
Is something wrong?

OEDIPUS

Please don't ask me.   1270

THESEUS
Tell me what all this is about.

OEDIPUS
I know now who this man is.

THESEUS
Who is he?
Who is it?
Speak!

OEDIPUS
Good king, it is my hateful son
whose words will wound me to the quick.

THESEUS
Surely it is possible to hear him out,
to listen without doing anything more.

OEDIPUS
Don't force me to do this.   1280
His very voice is hateful to me.

THESEUS
His prayers and supplications demand
that you show some respect for the god.

ANTIGONE
Listen to me, father. Though I am
young, let me try to persuade you.
Allow the man to satisfy himself
and the immortal God. Permit our brother
to come here to us. Nothing he says
can hurt you, and what's the harm
in hearing whatever he has to say?   1290
If he has wicked plans, his very words

will expose him. You are his father.
No matter what he has done to you
it is unjust to pay him back in kind.
Be merciful. Other men have fathered evil children,
and others have been racked with terrible rage.
And yet they listen and learn from their friends.
Think of the past, of all the sufferings
you endured because of your father and mother.
Think how evil always leads to more evil.   1300
Let your blind eyes remind you.
It is wrong for me to have to beg you.
You owe some kindness for kindness freely given.

OEDIPUS
Daughter, your words have moved me.
Your pleasure will be my pain, but let it be.
I ask you this much. If he comes here,
do not allow him to take control of me.

THESEUS
Once is enough, old man.
You already know that you are safe
for as long as the gods save me.   1310
(Exit Theseus and soldiers.)

CHORUS
Any man unhappy with his life,
his modest portion of good and ill,
will hunger for much more, for great things,
for pleasure without measure, gifts beyond counting.
And such a one, living to be old
will learn the many lessons of pain
as all pleasures diminish and disappear,
as life, itself, shrivels and fades
to black night at the end,
without end, without songs and dances,   1320

with only darkness and silence there.
Best of all is not to be born,
but to him who has come to see the light
the next best thing is early death.
Airheaded youth with all its foolishness
gives way to evil and to hardship,
to quarrels and murder, war and rage,
and, last of all, to ruined old age,
weak and alone, much despised
with pain as your only friend.   1330
This bitter old man is battered down
(as am I, as are we all),
like a wild shore tortured by a storm,
like rocks in the surf and wind.

ANTIGONE
Father, here comes the man
you are waiting for, alone and weeping.
(Enter Polynices, weeping.)

OEDIPUS
Who is it?

ANTIGONE
He is the one we spoke of.
Polynices has come here.

POLYNICES
Why am I crying, sisters?   1340
Is it all because of my own sorrows?
Or is it the spectacle of my father,
dirty and disheveled, an exile
in a foreign land, blind and terrible to behold?
I have learned these things too late.
I confess that I have greatly offended against you
by failing to offer you my support.

Others have told you, but hear it now
from me. God tempers justice with mercy,
and so be merciful to me, father.   1350
I can do nothing worse than I have.

Speak, father, say something to me.
Please give me some kind of answer.
Don't send me away without one word.
Tell me, at least, the rage you feel.

Daughters of Oedipus, my dear sisters,
speak to our father, plead my case.
Let him not disgrace me
in the eyes of the gods.

ANTIGONE

Speak for yourself, brother.   1360
Tell him what it is you want.
Sometimes a wealth of words
can waken the hardest heart.

POLYNICES

Well, then, I'll follow your advice
and speak for myself, first calling on
the God for whose sake the king of the land
has allowed me to come here and given me
his pledge for my safety, coming and going.
And now I want to tell you, father,
why I am here. I have been sent   1370
in exile from my native land
because, being the firstborn son,
I justly claimed the right to the throne.
It was Eteocles, my younger brother,
who drove me out of the city,
not by an argument or an act of force
but by persuading the city.
I blame it on the curse we bear.

When I came to Dorian Argos,
I took Adrastus, the king,   1380
as my father-in-law and I found
many allies among the finest families,
men honored for their great courage,
who will join me now with seven troops
of spearmen in an attack on Thebes,
there either to die in our good cause
or to drive out those who have done these things.

And why have I come here now?
To beg you, father, on behalf
of myself and my allies.   1390
Who are we? All brave men:
Amphiaraus, best in battle, able to read
the subtlest omens; Tydeus,
the Aetolian, son of Oeneus;
next Eteoclus, born and raised
in Argos; and Hippomedon fourth,
sent by Talaus, his father;
and the fifth of these is Capaneus
who has sworn to burn Thebes to ashes;
sixth Parthenopaeus, mighty son   1400
of Atalanta; and last is I,
your son, child of an evil fate,
but your son nonetheless. It is I
who will lead the army of Argos against Thebes.
All of us pray to you, father, hoping
you will swallow your anger and give some favor
as I go forth to take revenge
against my brother and my country.
The oracles—believe them if you care to—
say that the side you take will prevail.   1410
For the sake of the holy fountains
and the gods of all our race, I beg
you to hear me and help me, father.
We are exiles and strangers together.

We both of us depend on charity
and the kindness of strangers. Our fate
is much the same. Meanwhile the tyrant
at home takes pleasure in mocking us both.
If you will only choose to stand by me,
I shall win an easy victory   1420
and bring you home to your own place.
If you want what I want,
then all these things will be done.
But without you, father, I am lost
before I even begin.

CHORUS

For the sake of Theseus, old man,
say what you have to and send him away.

OEDIPUS

Friends and guardians of this place,
if it were not for the judgment of Theseus,
this man would never hear the sound of my voice.   1430
Now let him enjoy the privilege
and hear words that will not make him glad.
You are the one who sat on the throne
where your brother now wears the crown;
and you are the one who drove me out
to leave me as I am. You wept
like a child when you saw me now,
now that you, too, have earned your share
of woe. There is no good reason for tears.
I must endure for as long as I live,   1440
but I will always think of you
as my murderer. It's to you I owe
this misery. You cast me out, you made
me into a wandering beggarman.
Without my daughters to look after me
I would surely be dead now.

They saved me, these two, nurses,
more men than women, more my sons
than either you or your ill-begotten brother.

God is watching you and sees   1450
that your army will never conquer Thebes.
You will never destroy that city.
You and your brother will die a bloody death.
I have often cursed you and now again
I summon the power of that curse
to teach you the lesson of respect,
to honor your parents even in dishonor,
to be faithful as my daughters are.
May all my curses overcome your prayers.
May Justice share the throne of God.   1460
Go now! Blind as I am, I spit
on your name and call down my curse
against you: that you will lose
your war with Thebes and never will return
to Argos; that your brother will kill you
even as your hand will murder him.
These are the things I pray for. I petition
the darkest underworld to take you home.
I call upon the goddesses living here
and the god of war who taught you to hate.   1470
And now that you have heard my voice,
go and tell the Thebans and your friends
these are the blessings your father bestows.

CHORUS
Polynices, we can offer you no comfort.
The time has come for you to go.
POLYNICES
Pity my wasted coming.
Pity my good friends.
I can't speak of any of this

to them. I can't turn back.
I must go on and die without a word.   1480
Sisters, if his curses come to pass
and if you ever come home to Thebes,
promise, I beg you, to bury me
with fitting and honorable funeral rites.
Add that deed to your well-earned honor.

ANTIGONE

Polynices, I ask you, hear me now.

POLYNICES

Dearest sister, tell me what it is.

ANTIGONE

Turn back to Argos with your army.
Do not destroy yourself and Thebes.

POLYNICES

But if I fail my allies now,   1490
how can I hope to lead them again?

ANTIGONE

What is the true cause of your fury?
What good can come from the death of Thebes?

POLYNICES

Shame and dishonor inspire me.
And I hate the laughter of my brother.

ANTIGONE

See how you're making your father's curse
come true. The two of you are doomed to die.

POLYNICES

If that is truly his desire,
then we shall certainly confirm it.

ANTIGONE
>Who will obey you   1500
>when they hear your father's curse?

POLYNICES
>Not one word of this bad news.
>A good commander tells his men
>only the news that's fit to know.

ANTIGONE
>Then I take it, brother,
>your mind is firmly made up.

POLYNICES
>Nothing can be changed. I must go
>on, forward in spite of my father's curse.
>May God bless you and give you
>good fortune, if you'll do what I asked.   1510
>Farewell, sisters, you will never see
>my face among the living again.
>I do not ask your pity or your tears.

ANTIGONE
>Who would not mourn for you, brother,
>when certain death is waiting for you?

POLYNICES
>I am ready to die if I have to.

ANTIGONE
>You can live if you'll only do
>as I have said to you.

POLYNICES
>I can't be persuaded.
>Let it be.   1520

ANTIGONE
>   Then it is certain
>   that I shall lose you.

POLYNICES
>   All things are in the hands
>   of the gods, the gods to whom I pray
>   for your sake. May my sisters
>   never again know evil and misfortune.
> *(Exit Polynices. Thunder and lightning begin and continue until Theseus*
> *appears.)*

CHORUS
>   More evil and now the curse
>   of a terrible fate unless
>   some ineffable destiny
>   is finding its way to fruition.   1530
>   The gods do nothing without purpose.
>   Time is the witness of all things.
>   Some are rising, some must fall.
>   Hear God's thunder crack the sky.

OEDIPUS
>   Children, daughters, if any man is here,
>   send him to bring Theseus to us.

ANTIGONE
>   Why do you summon him now, father?

OEDIPUS
>   Hear the winged thunder of God
>   who will soon come to carry me down
>   to the underworld. Bring Theseus now!   1540

CHORUS
>   Hear the huge voice of God.
>   My hair stands up in dreadful fear.
>   My spirit shrinks inside itself and hides

when lightning blazes in the sky.
What is the meaning and the cause?

OEDIPUS

Children, according to prophecy
my life is nearly at the end.

ANTIGONE

How do you know that?
What tells you so?

OEDIPUS

I know the truth.   1550
Someone must quickly bring the king.

CHORUS

And still these thunders crash and roar.
O God, we ask you to be kind,
be merciful to us and, if you will,
forgive us for our sins.
Hear us, Lord, in our solemn prayer.

OEDIPUS

Has the king come yet?
Will he find me still alive
with my mind clear
and my words coherent?   1560

ANTIGONE

What is it that you want to do?

OEDIPUS

In return for his loving kindness
I will give him the blessing I promised.

CHORUS

Come, our son, our king.
Leave the rocky ritual place

where you offer oxen to Poseidon.
Come now, as we call you
for the sake of the blind stranger
and his wish to give you and the city
a just return for hospitality.   1570
Come quickly, we pray you.
(Enter Theseus.)

THESEUS

Why are all of you shouting?
What's the meaning of all this noise
and clamor? Is it the familiar
thunder and lightning of God?

OEDIPUS

My lord, I rejoice you are here.
The gods have given you good luck.

THESEUS

What do you want to tell me,
son of Laius?

OEDIPUS

My life is almost over, and I want   1580
to honor my promise before I die.

THESEUS

What tells you that your death is near?

OEDIPUS

The gods themselves have brought
this news by signs and portents.

THESEUS

And what are these signs, old man?

OEDIPUS

>Continual thunder and the bolts
>of lightning hurled by the hand of God.

THESEUS

>I believe you. You have never yet
>made a false prophecy.
>Tell us what must be done.   1590

OEDIPUS

>Son of Aegeus, permit me now
>to tell you what is coming to this city,
>this city beyond all age and decay.
>In a little while I will go by myself,
>with no one leading or guiding, to the place
>where I will die. You must never reveal
>to anyone else where this place is.
>Honor and preserve the secret
>and you will always be better defended
>than by swords and shields and many allies.   1600
>You alone will learn the mysteries,
>all the sacred words and forbidden things.
>I will never tell these things to anyone
>else, not citizens, not my own children.
>And you must keep the secret, too,
>until your end, and only then tell your heir.
>And likewise he will tell his own successor.
>And so it is the city will always be safe
>against all enemies, children of the dragon.
>Many the city that has slowly turned   1610
>from virtuous authority to arrogant vice.
>The gods always take note of this madness.
>May you never have to pay that price.

>All that I'm saying you already know.
>And now let us go to the proper place.

The power of the gods is present
and there is no time left to wait.
Come, daughters, follow me this way.
I whom you led now act as your guide.
Come without touching me, and let me be   1620
to seek and find the holy ground
where I can hide and rest in earth.
Come this way! Hermes and Persephone,
point the way in darkness for me.

O light without shining
I can feel your warmth
and presence one last time.
Now I will enter the dark underworld.
Blessings on all you good people.
I pray you will remember me well.   1630
May you have good fortune and prosperity.
(Exeunt Oedipus, Antigone, Ismene, Theseus.)

CHORUS

It is right for us to pray
to the dark goddesses and to
the Lord of the darkest underworld.
Be merciful to this stranger.
Let him be spared the worst.
He has suffered more than most.
Let the just gods be merciful.

We call upon the powers of hell
and especially to the great beast   1640
who, snarling, guards the gates.
Let Oedipus arrive among the dead
safely, and let him go to sleep
without fear in everlasting night.
Let him finally rest in peace.
(Enter Messenger.)

MESSENGER
> Citizens, the long and short
> of my news is that Oedipus is dead.
> But the whole truth of what has happened
> is not so simple as my words may seem.

CHORUS
> Is the old man dead?   1650

MESSENGER
> All that is altogether certain is
> that he has departed this life.

CHORUS
> Did he die without pain,
> thanks be to God? What happened?

MESSENGER
> This is a great cause for wonder.
> You know how he left here without a guide
> to help him, leading the others with him.
> He came to the hill with the steps
> of brass and stopped on one of the paths
> branching out from there, near to the basin   1660
> that marks the covenant of Theseus and Pirithous.
> Between there and the Thorician rock,
> he sat down by the hollow pear tree
> and removed his filthy clothing,
> calling on his daughters to command
> them to bring him water for bathing
> and libation from a stream nearby.
> They went to the hill of Demeter
> and did their duty, bringing the water
> to bathe him and dressing him   1670
> in appropriate and customary garments.
> When everything was done as he wished

and all his commands carried out,
God made the thunder roll again,
and the maidens trembled with fear
and fell to their knees beside him,
weeping as if their hearts were broken.
Then he took them in his arms and spoke:
"Daughters, this is the day of my death.
All things have come to this end   1680
and you'll never have to care for me again.
It was never an easy task, I know;
and now one word, love, will set you free
from the yoke of your pain and grief.
No one could have loved you more than I.
Go forth and live your lives freely without me."

So then, clinging to each other,
all of them were sobbing. But when
they ceased and there was silence,
suddenly a voice called out   1690
and all of us shook with fear:
"Oedipus, why are you waiting?
You have delayed too long.
It is time for you to go."
He knew it was a God speaking
and he called for Theseus to come to him.
When Theseus came near he said:
"Prince of this city, my good friend,
take the hands of my children,
and you, daughters, take his hands.   1700
Promise me, lord, you will never betray them
and that you will do what's best for them."
Then Theseus, as befitting a good king,
promised to do the things he was asked to.
Next Oedipus placed his frail old hands
on the heads of his children
and spoke to them gently, saying:

"Daughters, bear this with nobility.
Leave now, don't try to see what may not be seen
or to hear the words which are sacred   1710
and secret. Go now at once,
leaving Theseus here alone to learn
all that is about to happen."

All of us heard him say those words.
Then with his weeping daughters we left
and in a little while turned around.
The old man was no longer there. The king
stood alone, shading his eyes as if
to cover them against a fearful vision.
But after a moment and without a word   1720
he knelt down in prayer to earth and sky.
How the old man died no one knows
except for the king. There was no thunder
or lightning, no whirlwind off the sea.
Maybe an escort of the gods
came and took him away, or else
the dark world simply opened up its doors.
This much is certain, he was taken
away from us without more pain and suffering.
This death was clearly a kind of miracle.   1730
If any of you think I am a fool,
I would be a fool to argue with you.

CHORUS
Where are his daughters?
Where are the others?

MESSENGER
They're coming.
Listen and you can hear
the loud sound of their lamentations.
(Enter Antigone and Ismene.)

ANTIGONE
    We are left behind to live and lament
    the dark curse in our family blood.
    We have suffered for the sake   1740
    of our father, he who has gone,
    leaving us an inheritance
    beyond all understanding.

CHORUS
    Tell us what happened.

ANTIGONE
    Friends, we can only guess at that.

CHORUS
    Has he truly gone?

ANTIGONE
    Gone as any of us would wish to go.
    Neither the gods of war nor of the sea
    took him away, but something else
    inexplicable, ineffable, wholly mysterious.   1750
    And here we are lost without him.
    Sister, how can we keep living
    and wandering across strange lands and seas?

ISMENE
    Let the underworld take me, too,
    so that I can share our father's death.
    I would rather die than try to go on.

CHORUS
    Sisters, good daughters, be brave.
    Accept the terms of your fate
    without too much passion.
    No one can ever blame you.   1760

ANTIGONE

Strange how I now regret
what was painful at the time.
Whatever was bitter, I found sweet
when I held my father in my arms.
O father, you who are now clothed
in the darkness of the underworld,
even there you will feel our undying love.

CHORUS

He lived out his life and time.

ANTIGONE

He lived and died as he wished to.

CHORUS

How is that?   1770
What do you mean?

ANTIGONE

He died in another country,
just as he chose to do,
finding his grave in the shade,
leaving tearful mourners behind.
How I weep for the loss of you,
father, even as I grow weary
of the weight of my grief.
You died as you wanted, among strangers.
Why couldn't I die here, too?   1780

ISMENE

What kind of future waits for you and me,
fatherless and so far from home?

CHORUS

His ending was a happy one.
And you have grieved enough.
There is never any safety from misfortune.

ANTIGONE
Sister, let us go there again.

ISMENE
Why should we do that?

ANTIGONE
I have a powerful longing to go.

ISMENE
A longing for what?

ANTIGONE
To see the grave in the earth.   1790

ISMENE
Whose grave?

ANTIGONE
Our father's.

ISMENE
But that is forbidden.

ANTIGONE
Don't talk to me of right and wrong.

ISMENE
But even so, there is . . .

ANTIGONE
There is what?

ISMENE
There is no grave.
He descended alone into the dark.

ANTIGONE
> Then take me there and kill me too.

ISMENE
> What's to become of us?   1800
> How can we endure?

CHORUS
> Fear not. Do not be afraid.

ANTIGONE
> But where can I ever take refuge?

CHORUS
> More than once you have overcome . . .

ANTIGONE
> What?

CHORUS
> You have overcome misfortune.

ANTIGONE
> I do not think so.

CHORUS
> What are you thinking?

ANTIGONE
> How will we ever return home?

CHORUS
> Do not seek to return there.   1810

ANTIGONE
> We are deeply in trouble.

CHORUS

You have passed through troubles before.

ANTIGONE

And now things are worse than ever.

CHORUS

It's true, you have voyaged
on a sea of troubles.

ANTIGONE

Almighty God, where can we turn?
What gods can keep hope alive in our hearts?
(Enter Theseus.)

THESEUS

No more grieving, sisters.
We must not mourn for one
to whom the gods have been generous   1820
for fear that we will anger them.

ANTIGONE

Son of Aegeus, we call on you.

THESEUS

What is it you want from me?

ANTIGONE

To see our father's burial place
with our own eyes.

THESEUS

That is not permitted.

ANTIGONE

What do you mean?

THESEUS
> Your father made me promise
> never to go near the place again,
> nor to tell anyone how to find   1830
> the sacred tomb that's now his home.
> Zeus and his blessed son, protector
> of promises and pledges, heard me
> swear my solemn oath on this.

ANTIGONE
> If this was my father's pleasure,
> then we shall rightly honor it.
> But, please, sir, send us home
> to Thebes, where we may yet
> somehow or other prevent
> the bloody war that will be   1840
> the death of our brothers.

THESEUS
> I will do that and also
> anything else that I can do
> for the sake of your dead father.
> As long as I live, I'll keep my word.

CHORUS
> Call this the end of grieving.
> Lift up your hearts.
> We are all in the hands of the God.

Antigone

Translated by
Kelly Cherry

Translator's Preface

Two opposing propositions engage each other in a contest that can have no winner since what would be won is a balance between them: authority versus the individual conscience; the State versus the family; justice versus mercy; respect for logic versus respect for the limits of logic. For this last we might say instead "the gods," for the gods remind us that what we cannot control we must accept, that although a man may govern a state, no man governs himself.

As the play opens, the attacking Argive army is in retreat from Thebes. The two sons of Oedipus, Polynices and Eteocles, lie dead on the battlefield, one having lost his life in a traitorous attempt to gain the crown, the other having died defending it. Creon, brother of Jocasta and now the new king of Thebes, declares that he will rule his torn State in its best interests. He explains that the State should and will receive priority over personal concerns or attachments, including his own; the good of the all is more important than the good of any one. Therefore, he decrees, Polynices is to remain unburied, unprotected by the rituals that would secure him an afterlife in the underworld. Eteocles, a true Theban hero, will be buried with due military honors.

The brothers' two sisters, Antigone and Ismene, discuss how to respond to the decree; Antigone feels she must do what she believes is right and provide for Polynices the burial her uncle would deny him. As Creon is the father of her betrothed, her decision imperils not only herself and her sister but her fiancé, who is now in an untenable position between his beloved and his father. Almost immediately, then, the tragedy is set in motion. A translator entering this play steps off a cliff and discovers that from here on things can go in only one direction: down.

With a swiftness that takes us by surprise no matter how many times we have read, listened to, or seen the play we are pulled down from the triumph of Theban victory over the Argive army to the shattering conclusion. It is as if the play exerts a gravity we cannot resist, and of course it does. We are compelled by the tensile strength of Greek tragedy, powerless to refuse its embrace.

Desiring a similar economy in the English translation, I collapsed the odes into sonnets. The images and ideas of the odes are still here, in the sonnets; only the traditional rhetoric of translation is gone. For example,

> Think
> of the Wind-God's daughter, whose husband imprisoned her near
> where the Iron Rocks guard the Bosporus.
> Her young sons' stepmother gouged out their eyes, jealous.
>
> (702–5)

These three lines replace two strophes in Fitts and Fitzgerald's version, twenty-five lines (1066–90) in Fagles's. I was willing to relinquish their more leisurely retellings of an old, analogical story for a compression that keeps the emphasis on the play's plot line. "The Plot, then, is the first principle, and, as it were, the soul of a tragedy" (Aristotle, *Poetics*).

For similar reasons, I generally used a five-stress line. There is in this play a marvelous ability to move between the gritty diction of domestic realism and grand poetic statement. The five-stress line, often broken between speakers, supports these transitions in English. Free verse does, also, of course, but I wanted both the dignity of pentameter and the impactful density of speech that must say what it has to say within a certain amount of time, that urgency, that necessity.

In the convention of witches and soothsayers, Tiresias' lines employ end rhyme, as do Creon's when he converses with Tiresias.

The extension of Antigone's speech as she is led off to her tomb (665–80), often omitted as spurious, is included here, but I agree that it might have been dropped. Antigone is loyal to Polynices not because he cannot be replaced by another brother born to her dead parents but because she believes loyalty to one's family is a birthright, granted by the gods, and, as gifts granted by gods always are, a principle of dutiful action. "What right / has Creon to make me abandon my family?" (39–40).

That Antigone, whose father was her half-brother and whose mother was her grandmother, should be willing to risk everything to uphold the sanctity of the family is ironic or inevitable, depending on one's point of view. I do not think that she longed to be a martyr. (Male translators seem to think she did.) (Nor do I see Creon as a murdering tyrant, unless Governor George Bush, Jr., of Texas is a murdering tyrant. Creon is trying to adhere to the laws of the State, never mind that it was he who established the laws of the State.)

I have always loved Antigone, though she is not especially lovable, for her strength and clarity and dedication to principle. Growing up in a society in which women were either soft and subservient or failures at life, I loved Antigone as one whose death was an unretreating, almost aggressive affirmation of what she had stood for in life. She did not choose to die; she chose to act in accordance with her beliefs, and a world of men frightened by her independence put her to death. As a teenager, I even wished I had been named Antigone; friends, I figured, could call me Annie.

That fear of independent women saturates Creon's dialogue. Creon is threatened by the flood of feeling that would overwhelm him were he to let down his defenses for even a moment. I do not mean to reduce the play to feminism, though it is surely a feminist play. Rather, I think that it is here, in Creon's desperate faith in reason and fear of irrationality, represented for him by woman's close association with the mysteries of birth and death, that we come closest to the sense of dread that must have permeated life in ancient Greece. What must it be like to inhabit an Earth only just touched by the "rosy-fingered dawn"? The wind and rain; the rocks and sea; the darkness of the grave, and the fire down below that could erupt and wreak havoc, visiting hell on earth, no matter where people were in their lives, about to marry or running a business or adding onto the house—imagine living that near to the edge of the unknown.

You could take a step and find yourself falling from a cliff.

Haemon, in love with and admiring of Antigone, practices the art of suasion on his father, flattering him into a position of confidence from which he can relax his adherence to the letter of the law. But as the underside of their discussion works its way to the spoken surface Creon understands that Haemon's mollifying speech "was nothing but a plea for her" (562). The measured lines of their dialogue have unraveled into a galloping match of wits, and Haemon hits his father where it hurts him most, telling him, "At least I have / not been taken in by spurious logic" (560–61).

The father wants the boy to be a man; the boy *is* a man, but the father is too afraid of his own capacity for feeling—which he identifies with femininity—to recognize it. Beginning in apparent amity, the scene ends in explosive rage. We all know how this goes: a stress fracture in the structure of a family gives way to expose an underlying flaw, and quicker than anyone would have predicted everything goes to hell.

Stichomythic dialogue that moves like argument (the Platonic dialogues use this technique), each speaker seizing the discourse from the other only to have it snatched back almost instantly, creates a rush like drugs, that sensation of tumbling downward through open air, earth rising toward the tragic characters like that "which was to be proved." Tragedy has a logic of its own, crashing into the conclusion already present in its premises.

> The past is always present; let it fall
> to the bottom of the ocean, a storm will stir
> black depths as if rain were a waterfall,
> waves heaving sand, ferrying the past ashore. (446–49)

What was needed to prevent the tragedy was a balance between two opposing views, but where can anyone find compromise between absolutes? Antigone's position makes sense—it is a position, for what Creon takes to be irrational feeling is for Antigone a premise (the gods) and a deduction (obedience)—and we sympathize with her; but Creon's position also makes sense, and by play's end we sympathize with him too. This is to say, I imagine, that even today we are vicariously the chorus, wavering and confused, unsteady and susceptible, weak, unheroic, alive, hanging on and getting by.

Cast

ANTIGONE, daughter of Oedipus and Jocasta
ISMENE, sister of Antigone
CHORUS OF THEBAN ELDERS
CHORAGOS, leader of the Chorus
CREON, king of Thebes, uncle of Antigone and Ismene
SENTRY
HAEMON, son of Creon and Eurydice
TIRESIAS, blind prophet
MESSENGER
EURYDICE, wife of Creon
NONSPEAKING
    Guards
    Attendants
    Boy, guide to Tiresias

(Thebes, in front of the royal palace of Creon. Antigone and Ismene emerge from the central door.)

ANTIGONE
    Ismene, darling sister, you must have noticed,
    once or twice, how we have had to pay
    for our father's sins. I mean, you name it,
    we've had to endure it. Now this. And why?
    For what?
                Oh, haven't you heard about this latest
    proclamation?
                Or do you just not care!

ISMENE
    Heard what, Antigone? All I know is,
    we've lost both our brothers in a single day.
    I heard the Argive army fled in the night.
    I've heard nothing else, no news good or bad.   10

ANTIGONE

> I thought that might be the case. That's why
> I wanted you to come outside with me,
> so I can tell you.

ISMENE

> What's wrong? Why are you whispering?

ANTIGONE

> What's wrong? How about our brothers being
> dead! How about one being buried
> with full honors while the other's treated
> like a traitor! Eteocles deserved
> his soldier's funeral but— Creon's declared
> that Polynices may not be buried or mourned.
> His body must lie out in the open, like carrion.   20
> The vultures will feast on him. It's horrible!
>
> At whom is this law aimed, if not at us?
>
> They also say that Creon's on his way
> here to make a public announcement about
> this, and that he's so hellbent on it,
> he swears anyone who dares to go against him
> will be put to death by stoning in the town square.
>
> That's it. That's what I had to tell you. Now
> you get to show the kind of stuff you're made of.

ISMENE

> Antigone, you're crazy! What can I do?   30

ANTIGONE

> You can make up your mind if you'll help me
> or not.

ISMENE

Help you do what? What do you mean?

ANTIGONE

Help me to bury our brother. I need your help
to lift his body.

ISMENE

Bury him! But you
just said that Creon has forbidden anyone
to bury him!

ANTIGONE

He's my brother. Yours too,
in case you have forgotten.
Nobody
is going to be able to say I betrayed
my own brother.

ISMENE

You'd break the law?

ANTIGONE

What right
has Creon to make me abandon my family?   40

ISMENE

Sister, remember what happened to our father!
How he was shunned, disgraced, and, overcome
with self-loathing, condemned himself to blindness.
Remember Mother. When she learned she was also
his mother, she hanged herself. And don't forget
our brothers killed each other. Think about
the fact that we're all that's left of our family.
If we went against Creon, would we not die
the worst deaths yet?

We're just women, you know,
not powerful enough to go up against men.   50
Have you forgotten that the strong control
the weak? We have to obey Creon's orders,
this one and any others. I will ask the dead
to forgive me for obeying the law. It would be
a grave mistake to do anything else.

ANTIGONE

Forget it, Is. If that is how you feel,
I wouldn't let you come if you begged to.
You can go do whatever you want to do;
I'll bury him by myself. So what if I die!
It's for a good cause. I'll lie next to him   60
and make him happy forever, for that's how long
death lasts.
            You do what you want, since it's obvious
that you don't care about doing what's right.

ISMENE

                              I do,
but I am not willing to do what's wrong—
to break the law.

ANTIGONE

                That's an excuse.
                        I'm going.
I'll bury my darling brother myself.

ISMENE

                        My sister,
I'm so afraid for you! You're so reckless.

ANTIGONE

Don't worry about me. You have your*self*
to think about.

ISMENE

>At least keep it quiet.
Don't tell anyone! Neither will I, I promise.   70

ANTIGONE

Oh, go ahead and tell the whole city!
You'd better—imagine how they'll all feel
if they find out that you knew all along.

ISMENE

You're so fired up, but you ought to be
numb with fear.

ANTIGONE

>I'll be doing right by those
I should do right by.

ISMENE

>If you can do it,
but I don't think you can.

ANTIGONE

>I'll do my best.

ISMENE

It's pointless to attempt the impossible.

ANTIGONE

Leave me alone, Ismene. Lord! Your words
are so appalling, they will make me hate   80
you, and the dead will turn in their graves.
Let me do what I have to do. I'm not
afraid. If I must die, at least I won't
die the worst of deaths—a death without
honor.

ISMENE

        Do what you have to do. You're making
a mistake, but no one can say you're not loyal
to those who love you.
(Exits into the palace. Antigone exits. Chorus enters from left.)

CHORUS OF ELDERS

        The eye of day is opening, the sun
gazing upon the Seven Gates of Thebes.
Streaming across the swirling Dirce, light   90
makes a white-hot blaze of gleaming shields,
the Argive army in retreat,

CHORAGOS

                    an eagle
screaming insults as it attacked, set loose
by Polynices, with massed shields like white wings,
with every helmet bristling like the crest
of a bird of prey.

CHORUS

            The army gathered at
our gates, with spears as sharp as snapping beaks,
attacked at night, but was thrown back before
they could satisfy their thirst for blood,
or touch the crown of circling towers.
                       Thrown back—   100
and as they fled, the great Theban army,
like some Leviathan, a dragon, breathed
terror at their backs, the roar of war.

CHORAGOS

        For Zeus despises pride, the brag and swagger
of men, and when the Argive army stormed
the city walls, he struck the first man down
with a bolt of lightning as golden as Argive armor.
We heard the man's proud boast become a scream

as, spotlit by the torch intended for
the devastation of Thebes, he fell to earth—   110
the fall that follows pride, indeed. And then,
it seemed that Ares himself dealt the blows
that laid the others low—as low as dust.

CHORAGOS
   The seven captains at the seven gates
   retreated in defeat. None but the two
   brothers, each a mirror of the other
   in life and death, came face to face and hand
   to hand in combat.

CHORUS
                    But, in our morning
   of glorious victory, let the city sing
   for joy! We'll dance away all thoughts of war;   120
   our temples will be filled with hymns of praise;
   oh, the celebration will continue
   far into the night.

CHORAGOS
                    But look! Creon,
   our new king, crowned by circumstance,
   is drawing near. I wonder why. And why
   does he summon us, the elders, to his side?
(Enter Creon.)

CREON
   Gentlemen, I am pleased to be able
   to tell you that our ship of state, which had
   foundered in the recent storms, has arrived
   in port safely, thank God. I've summoned you here   130
   because I know I can count on you: You proved
   your loyalty to Laius; when he died,
   you never hesitated in your duty
   to Oedipus; and when Oedipus died,

you were loyal to his royal heirs.
Sadly, the boys have killed each other in battle,
and now it's I who must assume the throne.
I know, of course, that no ruler's entitled
to loyalty until he has been tested.
Still, I can promise you that I will do   140
whatever's best for Thebes; I've nothing but
serious contempt for any leader who
would place himself—or his friend, for that matter—
above the State. By God, I shall speak out
when speaking out is needed; and I'd never
make any deal behind the scenes with an enemy
of the State, knowing that all of Thebes is in
the same boat, so to speak—this ship of state.
Private connections cannot take priority
over the public good.

                Consequently,   150
I've reached the following decision regarding
Oedipus' sons: Eteocles,
who died fighting for his country, is
to be buried with full military honors,
as is usual for heroic casualties;
but his brother, Polynices, who returned
from exile to wage war against his homeland,
who was determined to wreak his vengeance
on his own people and against his father's gods
—no one is to bury him or mourn for him.   160
His corpse will lie out in the open, and dogs
and crows will do with it what dogs and crows
do.

     And this is a command.

                While I am king,
traitors will not be honored with heroes. Rather,
the man who is ever ready to lay down
his life for his country will have my respect
alive, and dead, my reverence.

CHORUS

                    The card
is yours to call, Creon son of Menoeceus.
Your word is law.

CREON

               I take it, then, you'll do
as I say.

CHORAGOS

          We're old. Let the younger men   170
execute this particular order.

CREON

     That is not what I meant. In fact, sentries
have already been appointed.

CHORAGOS

                 But then—
what exactly are you telling us to do?

CREON

     Not to interfere.

CHORAGOS

           We're old, not crazy.

CREON

     I see you take my point—that the penalty
is death. Yet you would be surprised how many
men will give up their lives for mere money.
(Enter Sentry.)

SENTRY

     Sir, I am not going to pretend I rushed
to get here, because I didn't. Every time   180
I thought about what I have to tell you,

I almost stopped and turned around. A voice
in my head kept saying, "You fool, why run
to meet your fate?" And then—"But if Creon
hears about this from someone else, you'll be
in even bigger trouble." So here I am—
though I managed to make a short journey long—
because, well, whatever happens, happens.

CREON

What are you trying to say, man? Speak your mind!

SENTRY

I didn't do it, I didn't even see   190
who did it. So please don't blame the messenger
for the news.

CREON

You sure can beat about the bush.

SENTRY

Any bringer of bad news knows enough
to come in fear, and trembling.

CREON

Nonsense. *Out*
with it, and you can go—

SENTRY

I guess the news
has to be delivered: The corpse is buried;
just very recently, someone sprinkled
dust upon it, performing the ritual—
and vanished.

CREON

And who was the man who dared
to do this deed?

SENTRY

               I swear that I don't know!   200
You have to believe me! There wasn't even a trace—
not a sign of digging, not a wheel track,
nothing to give away who had done it.
When the morning watch showed up, their corporal
pointed to it. We were all stunned.
                      The body
had been—not interred, but sifted over
with light dust; not really buried but covered,
as if to protect the body from blasphemy.
And not a sign of wild dogs or jackals.
And then all hell broke loose, everyone accusing   210
everyone, and each of us defending himself,
but there was no evidence to prove
any of us guilty. So finally,
someone said something that shut us all up:
You had to be informed of what had happened.
We threw the dice, and I was unlucky.
So here I am, and I have to say that
I don't want to be here any more
than you want me to be here: nobody
likes bad news.

CHORAGOS

             I've been thinking, this could be   220
the work of the gods, Creon . . .

CREON

                  Oh, for God's sake,
I swear I'm beginning to think you're all senile.
And *why* would the gods reward a dead man
who served them by looting their temples, burning
their altars, wrecking their shrines, not to mention
spoiling their land and breaking their laws?
                     Maybe
you think the gods love evil instead of good?

No, from the beginning I've known that there are those
who don't approve of me or my decree.
They scheme and whisper. In all likelihood,   230
they bribed my own sentries to bury the corpse.
Money! Men will do anything for it!

(to Sentry)

In the name of God, I promise you
that if you don't find out who disobeyed
my orders and bring him to me, you will beg
for death, because I will have you strung up alive.
A little discipline'll encourage you
to confess. You will tell us who it was
who paid you, and you'll learn the hard way that
money isn't always worth what you have   240
to do for it.

SENTRY

Sir, may I speak?

CREON

I can
hardly bear to listen to you.

SENTRY

Why?
Because you can't stand the sound of my voice,
or because you can't stand to hear the truth?

CREON

Don't tell me that you're going to analyze
me, now!

SENTRY

I'm just the messenger. I'm not
responsible for how you feel.

CREON

Good God,
does nothing shut you up? Get out of here—

SENTRY

So maybe I talk too much, but I haven't
done anything wrong.

CREON

The hell you haven't. As if   250
you haven't sold your soul for petty cash.

SENTRY

It's *bad news* when a leader jumps to conclusions.

CREON

Talk all you like, but if you don't bring me
the perp, you'll wish you had kept your trap closed.
(Turns sharply, exits.)

SENTRY

I hope somebody captures the son of a bitch,
but it won't be me. Thank God, I'm outta here.
(Exits.)

Ode to Man

CHORUS

Of all the wonders of the world, most wonderful
is man: On sea and land he travels freely,
a sailor, farmer, hunter of the bountiful
birds and wild beasts, and fish unswift to flee.   260
He conquers all—lion, horse, and ox,
and words, and ideas, even wind and weather.
Except for death, there is no plague or pox
he has not learned to steer clear of or endure.
His intelligence is marvelous,

and if he lives by the law, he'll do just fine,
but a mind that raises itself above all else,
that thinks it knows everything, will undermine
the absolute foundation of its world,
and ours.
(*Reenter Sentry, leading Antigone.*)

CHORAGOS
                    Annie? What brings you here, my child?   270

SENTRY
    Here's your traitor! We caught her in the act!
    So where is Creon? . . .

CHORAGOS
                            Headed right this way.
(*Enter Creon, with servants.*)

CREON
    What's going on?

SENTRY
                    You know, a man just never
    knows what the future will bring. I could have sworn
    nothing would bring me back here after what
    I went through the first time, but—looks like my luck's
    changed!
                    Here is your traitor—a woman! We caught her
    redhanded.
                    She's all yours, judge. Punish her
    as you like. This time, I'm gone for good.

CREON
                            This is
    Antigone. Why have you brought her here?   280

SENTRY

    She was covering the corpse of Polynices.
    Like I said.

CREON

             Are you insane? Have you any
    idea of what you're saying?

SENTRY

                  I saw her myself.
    That says it all.

CREON

             I want to hear details.

SENTRY

    Then here they are: With those threats of yours
    still ringing in my ears, I returned to my post.
    We swept away the dust, so the body was bared.
    The stink of it was strong, a smell of rotting.
    So we climbed a hill, keeping the body downwind.

    Now we kept guard, and we made sure nobody   290
    nodded off on the job. But nothing happened—
    not until noon, when suddenly the sky
    went black, as a dust storm blew up, like an explosion,
    uprooting trees and causing the earth to quake.
    We closed our eyes against the stinging wind—
    it was as if shattered glass was being thrown
    in our faces.
              When it was over and
    we opened our eyes again, we saw this woman.

    She was crying. All her work was undone.
    You know how when a mother bird discovers   300
    her nestlings stolen she will tear the air
    apart with her shocked and bitter cries?

Like that, this young woman wept, and begged
God above to curse the "grave-robbers"—
yours truly, of course—who had bared the body.
And then she poured a handful of dust on the body
and sprinkled wine, three times, as a libation.

We took her into custody, charging
her with treason. Even then, she was unafraid.
She denied nothing.
                 I must admit I'm relieved   310
she's willing to confess; it lets me off
the hook. I wish she didn't have to die,
but, well, better her than me.

CREON *(to Antigone)*
                     Look
me in the eye, girl! Is what this man says
true?

ANTIGONE
       Yes. All of it.

CREON *(to Sentry)*
                  You may go. And
don't forget that you're one lucky bastard.
(Exit Sentry. To Antigone)
       Now answer this question yes or no:
Were you aware that I had ordered that
your brother's body was to remain unburied?

ANTIGONE
       Yes. There was no one who didn't know.   320

CREON
       And you broke the law anyway?

ANTIGONE

I did.

I had to choose between your law and God's law,
and no matter how much power you have
to enforce your law, it is inconsequential
next to God's. His laws are eternal, not
merely for the moment. No mortal, not
even you, may annul the laws of God,
for they *are* eternal.

For example,
I knew that I must die whether I obeyed
your order or not. We will all die. And if   330
I die now, so what if it is early.
To someone as bereft as I am, death
is a friend. So you see, this death of mine
does not scare me, but if I abandoned my brother,
leaving his spirit to roam aimlessly
and alone forever, I would, myself,
suffer forever. This way, we will both
be at peace.

I realize that you
probably think I'm stupid, but then, why
should that worry me, since it seems to me   340
that if anyone's behaving stupidly here,
it's you.

CHORAGOS

Like father, like daughter, stubborn and
unyielding.

CREON

She will yield. She may not know it,
but a stiff will breaks first, the toughest iron
crumbles in fire, and wild horses are curbed
with a bit.

What gives her the right to be so proud?

She's doubly guilty—first of breaking the law
and then of boasting of it. If I let her go
unpunished, she might as well be the man
and I the woman. Niece, or even more   350
than that, she and her sister will both die.

(to servants)

Go; bring Ismene here; she's inside,
half hysterical and crying her eyes out.
Clearly, she's been in on this.

                    At least,

she hasn't tried to turn breaking the law
into something to brag about!

ANTIGONE

                    Creon—

what do you want now?

CREON

                  To see you pay
for your crime. That's all.

ANTIGONE

                Then go ahead: kill me.
I'm not any more interested in making
small talk with you than you can be with me,   360
but oh, what others would say—. If they weren't afraid,
everyone here would commend me for what I've done.
But it seems that only kings get to talk.

CREON

No one here would agree that you were right
to bury Polynices.

ANTIGONE

            Oh, they would,
but they don't dare.

CREON

     Aren't you ashamed to talk

treason?

ANTIGONE

   There should be nothing treasonable

in giving the dead their due.

CREON

       Oh yes? Well, Ann,

are you saying that Eteocles *wasn't*

your brother too?

ANTIGONE

     Of course he was.

CREON

       Then why   370

do you insult his memory?

ANTIGONE

     That's not

what he would think.

CREON

     I think he would, inasmuch

as you choose to honor a traitor alongside him.

ANTIGONE

 Polynices was his brother, traitor

or not.

CREON

   He plotted war against his country.

Eteocles defended his country.

ANTIGONE

But
some honors belong to all the dead.

CREON

You cannot
honor the wicked alongside the just.

ANTIGONE

Creon,
Uncle, how can any of us presume
to know what God thinks is wrong.

CREON

A traitor   380
remains a traitor, even dead.

ANTIGONE

Well, I
can't help but want to reconcile the dead
with the dead.

CREON

Then you will have your chance—
among the dead! I don't have to take this kind
of backtalk from a woman.
(*Enter Ismene, under guard.*)

CHORUS

Here is Ismene,
her eyes red from weeping.

CREON

In my house,
all the time, the two of you—bloodsuckers,
that's what you are, snakes in the grass—! You too,
Ismene. Do you deny it?

ISMENE

> I do not,
>
> and hope that Antigone will permit me to plead   390
> guilty.

ANTIGONE

> No, Ismene. You wouldn't help
> me when I asked for help, so now when you
> would ask to help, my answer's no.

ISMENE

> But now
> you need me, Ann. It breaks my heart to see
> you so alone, so lost and so at sea.

ANTIGONE

> Words—that's all you know. But God knows,
> if you really care about someone,
> you must do more than just talk about it.

ISMENE

> Why are you being so mean? I'm your sister,
> and I am willing to die to prove it. Let me.   400

ANTIGONE

> There's no need for you to die. One death
> is plenty, and if there's any honor attached
> to it, that honor's mine.

ISMENE

> But how will I go
> on living without you?

ANTIGONE

> Ask Creon, your new buddy.
> He seems to have all the answers.

ISMENE

                                        Oh, why
do you insist on making fun of me?

ANTIGONE

I wouldn't call it fun—I'm not exactly
falling over with laughter.

ISMENE

                            I'm ready to help.

ANTIGONE

If you really want to help, Ismene,
save yourself.
                    And don't worry—I won't   410
envy you your life.

ISMENE

                        You refuse to
let me die with you?

ANTIGONE

                            From the beginning
you chose to live.

ISMENE

                        You can't say I didn't
warn you.

ANTIGONE

            I wouldn't say that. I would say
that there are those who'll think you made the smarter
choice, and there are also those who'll think
that I was right.

ISMENE

                    According to Creon,
we are both guilty.

ANTIGONE
      You'll be all right, Is.
Creon won't kill you, and as for me, I am
already dead. I died the moment I   420
joined hands with the dead.

CREON *(to the Chorus)*
          Both of these women
are completely brainless. One's just lost her wits,
the other apparently never had any.

ISMENE
It would be insanity to be
sane in a world gone crazy as this.

CREON
          What's insane
is that you are siding with your sister.

ISMENE
But how would I go on living without
Antigone?

CREON
      As your sister said,
she's already dead, yet you're still alive.

ISMENE
Creon! Good God! She is your son's fiancée!   430

CREON
He can find another field to plow.
I'm not about to let him make the mistake
he'd be making if he married her.

ISMENE
But Haemon is in love with Antigone!
Oh Haemon, how your father hurts you!

CREON

                              Enough,
    I've had enough of your romantic tripe!

CHORAGOS

    Are you really going to make your son
    suffer like this?

CREON

                    It's not my fault. Blame death,
    not me. What stands in the way of this marriage
    is the law, not me.

CHORAGOS

                    Then she is going to die?   440

CREON

    You must be a genius, to have figured that
    out.
            —All right, let's get a move on!
(to guards)
    Take the both of them away and don't
    let them out of your sight. I wouldn't trust them
    even as far as I'd trust a condemned man.
(Exeunt Antigone and Ismene with guards.)

                Ode to Inescapable Sorrow
CHORUS

    The past is always present; let it fall
    to the bottom of the ocean, a storm will stir
    black depths as if rain were a waterfall,
    waves heaving sand, ferrying the past ashore.

    The past returns, and brings with it sorrow.   450
    The children endure the consequences of
    their parents' failings, today and tomorrow.
    Annie, like her father, will die for love.

The truly rich are those who do not suffer.
For everyone else, hope is the prophet of pain.
The flickering dreams of mortals are no match for
Fate's eternally shining, relentless sun.

Now Haemon, Creon's youngest son, approaches—
He knows? Has he come with curses? Reproaches?
(Enter Haemon.)

CREON
    We'll ask him.

               —Haemon, my son, I assume you've heard   460
    what Antigone has done, and the sentence
    I have been forced to pronounce on her.—Do you
    hate me?

HAEMON
          You are my father. A son cannot
    hate his father. I trust your judgment in
    all things, and I would never marry a woman
    of whom you did not approve.

CREON
             Good!
    That's how a son should feel about his father.
    This is what a man hopes for in a son,
    a kind of friend and colleague right from the jump,
    someone who'll be on his side, see his point   470
    of view. A son who insists on fighting with
    his father is nothing but trouble, and trouble everyone
    enjoys gossiping about. I'm glad to hear
    you haven't lost your head over this girl.
    There's nothing worse than life with the wrong woman.
    Antigone is cold and vicious—not
    much good in bed, I'll bet. Let her marry
    among the dead. That should suit her.

Haemon,
she is a traitor and must die, or else
I'd be a traitor too, and I will not   480
break my promise to the State.

I suppose
she'll claim that as my niece she should not be
put to death, but if I exempt my family
from the law, why should anyone else
be subject to it? It's important to people
to know that their leader's house is in order,
because if it's not, how can he be expected
to keep *their* house in order?

Discipline,
Haemon. A leader has to be obeyed
in everything. And it is the man   490
who knows how to obey who knows how to command.
He is the one who, in the thick of battle,
will stand his ground.

Anarchy!—that's what
makes armies flee and brings down city-states.
That's why we have to maintain authority,
especially where women are concerned.
Do you want the world to say you're pussywhipped?

CHORUS
Unless I am senile, what you say makes sense.

HAEMON
Father, I understand intelligence
is God's greatest gift, and that you're right   500
to want me not to behave stupidly.
I understand your reasoning. But there
are other ways of looking at a thing.
But sometimes we need someone else to show
them to us. Now, unlike you, I'm in a position

to hear what others think about all this.
No one else will tell you; they're too afraid.
But I can tell you, a lot of mumbling and grumbling
is going on, with people saying that
Antigone does not deserve to die.   510
In fact, they say, she should be praised for what
she did—covering her brother's body so
the dogs and vultures can not desecrate it.
Yes, that's what people are saying.
                              Now listen,
Father, no one means more to me than you.
You must know that. What son doesn't like
to see his father admired, just as a father
likes to see his son be successful?
I'm asking you, please consider their point
of view. No one is infallible.   520
A man who thinks he is—who thinks he's smarter
than everyone else—always falls on his face.
A reasonable man listens to reason.
                              I mean,
you know how a tree that bends in a flood
survives intact, while the tree that refuses
to give ground is uprooted?
                              Or—think about this:
if you never slacken your mainsail, you'll overturn
and then you can forget about the trophy.
Forget your anger! Let yourself be moved!
I know I'm young, but I am old enough   530
to know we all make mistakes. There's not
one of us who can't learn from others.

CHORAGOS
                              Creon,
listen to your son. He makes sense. And
Haemon, listen to your father. You both
make good points.

CREON

                    Are you telling me I should
let myself be educated by a mere boy?

HAEMON

    Father, all I'm asking for is justice.
    What matters is what I said. How old I am
    is beside the point.

CREON

                    Your point seems to be
that you think it's all right to break the law!   540

HAEMON

    I make no brief for anyone who breaks
    the law.

CREON

            Oh yes? Are you suggesting that
    Antigone is not a criminal?

HAEMON

    No one but you thinks she is a criminal.

CREON

    So I'm supposed to let the city decide
    just when a law is a law?

HAEMON

                    I think it's you
    who's talking like a child, now.

CREON

                        Am I to rule
the way others tell me to, or for myself?

HAEMON

    A State for one man's not much of a State.

CREON

    The State is the King!

HAEMON

              You'd be great as the monarch   550
    of a desert.

CREON

        My son, it seems, has chosen
    to side with a woman.

HAEMON

            Yes, well, that's true
    if *you're* a woman. I'm only thinking of what
    is best for you.

CREON

         "Best for me"!—for my son
    to contradict his father openly?

HAEMON

    I just don't want to see you make a mistake.

CREON

    And just how is it a mistake to uphold the law?

HAEMON

    There are laws, and laws. You are breaking
    natural law.

CREON

        Boy, have you ever been
    taken in by that girl!

HAEMON

At least I have   560
not been taken in by spurious logic.

CREON

Your speech was nothing but a plea for her.

HAEMON

And for you. And me. And the gods who dwell below.

CREON

She will never be your bride. Not while she's alive.

HAEMON

In that case, I will marry her in death.

CREON

Is that a threat?

HAEMON

I'm merely stating a fact.

CREON

You'll be sorry you ever took that tone
with me!

HAEMON

If you were not my father, I
would tell you what a damn fool you're being.

CREON

Don't you call me *father*! You're not man   570
enough—taking your orders from a woman!

HAEMON

Oh, that's right, no one's allowed to say anything
to you.

CREON

> This is the end. I will not tolerate
> insolence like this.

(to the servants)

> > Bring the girl out!
> Let's let him watch her die! Now! Right now!

HAEMON

> The hell you will. Watch you kill my love?
> You're mad. And you won't see my face again, either.

> Only another madman could stand the sight
> of you.

(Exit Haemon.)

CHORAGOS

> > He's gone!
> > > Creon, a young fellow
> is dangerous when he is as angry and   580
> upset as Haemon is.

CREON

> > Let him go.
> Let him dream up whatever harebrained plan
> he can to save his girlfriends. He won't succeed.

CHORAGOS

> Do you mean you're going to kill them both?

CREON

> You're right. Only the one who actually did it.

CHORAGOS

> And Antigone, what kind of death—

CREON

> She is to be taken out into
> the countryside and shut up in a vault

of stone. She'll have food, as is customary—
so no one will be able to say that the State   590
killed her.
      She will be at liberty
to pray all she wants to the king of death—
her kind of king. Maybe he will help her
escape.
      Or maybe, she'll finally figure out
it doesn't pay to care more for the dead
than for the living.
(Exit Creon.)

        Ode to Love

CHORUS
    We humans are the slaves of love, captured,
    even the strong and powerful among us,
    by the simplest touch or look, and lured
    into ruin by the way an evening breeze brushes   600
    a girl's soft cheek. It is you—*love*—that started
    uncivil war between father and son.
    It is you—*love*—hateful and hard-hearted,
    by whom even the wisest men are undone.
    Because of you, a man will give his life
    to a woman, give up everything,
    do anything to win her for his wife,
    will stop at nothing, not even dying.
    We ourselves would gladly renounce justice
    to save this girl. Our chorus has no voice.   610
(Antigone enters, under guard.)

ANTIGONE
    I come to say farewell, friends, and look
    at the sun one last time, before I sleep
    the sleep of death. I'm summoned to the dark.
    There will be no wedding song for me,
    no flowers strewn upon my marriage bed.
    It's Death I wed.

CHORUS
> Yet you die with honor.
And not by injury or disease—never
has another gone to her death alive.

ANTIGONE
> I keep thinking of Niobe, daughter
of Tantalus. They say that the cold stones   620
were twined around her as tight as ivy,
that she still waits alone through snow and rain,
crying. A living death, like mine.

CHORUS
> But she
was a daughter of the gods, and you
are not, and to die as she did confers
glory on you in the world and the underworld.

ANTIGONE
> I think that you are making fun of me.
Can't you wait till I'm dead? Oh friends,
oh fortunate, fair-weather friends! At least
the city itself, fountain and grove, knows   630
that I've been judged unjustly, pitilessly!
To be entombed alive! To be exiled
from both the living and the dead!

CHORUS
> There's no
help for it, for you went too far, and ran
up against the brick wall of justice. Almost,
it seems you've been trapped in your father's destiny.

ANTIGONE
> And now you have rubbed salt in my deepest wound,
my poor father's unlucky life, the error
that is bred into our bones, since it began

when he married his mother and I was born,   640
a sister and a daughter to the same man.
It is as if that marriage has killed mine,
as if my father-brother reaches his hand
from the grave to pull me down where I must belong.
(Enter Creon.)

CHORUS

It's true you only wished to pay your respects
to the dead, but you knew that you were disobeying
the king. You chose your fate.

ANTIGONE

                              Not even "fair-weather"—
I see I have no friends after all!
No one to weep for me, no husband. So
I will go, never to see the sun again.   650
How unloved I am, how alone!

CREON

If talking could delay death, the dying
would talk forever.
(to the servants)
                    Go on! Take her away!
You know what to do. Take her to the vault
and lock her up. Whether she chooses to live
or die is up to her: all we have done
is to exile her.

ANTIGONE

                    To the tomb, my sepulchral
bridal bed, my new and eternal home,
where I will greet my own family
once more, the last and youngest to arrive   660
in that place of the dead. And perhaps I will find
a warm welcome from my father and mother,
and Polynices—oh, you especially,

Polynices, for it was I who performed
the rites of burial for you.
                    For which,
I am to die. And yet I had no choice.
If you had been my child or my husband,
I would have had a choice. I might have found
another husband, had another child.
But because my father and mother are dead,   670
I cannot replace you with another brother.
In honoring you, I obeyed my conscience,
and Creon thinks this was a heinous crime
and has condemned me, like a common criminal,
to death. So that now the child, the husband
never will be mine—but, my God,
do I deserve this? Well, if I do,
I'll find out soon enough in the afterlife.
But if the truly guilty one is Creon,
I wish him nothing worse than he's wished me!   680

CHORAGOS
    She is as passionate, as determined
    as ever.

CREON
            Her guards must be tired of listening
    to her. That will teach them to be so slow
    about following my orders!

ANTIGONE
                            The voice of death—!

CREON
    You are right about that, anyway.

ANTIGONE
    Thebes, and the gods of Thebes, and leaders of Thebes,
    look on me as I, the last daughter

of your line of kings, am led away
to death. Remember how I suffered and
who punished me for fulfilling the laws of heaven.   690
(to guards)
I am ready. Let's go.
(Exit Antigone, under guard.)

Ode to Fate

CHORUS

No one, no mortal, is exempt from Fate.
Nothing can alter what the gods ordain.
About this, the gods are obdurate,
and even a royal princess cannot reign
over Fate. Remember Danaë—
like you, princess in a sunless cell.
She could not escape her destiny
though she was royal; though Zeus would love her well
and deeply. Think of the proud, mad king   700
whose blasphemy brought him to a dungeon, where
his curses echoed unheard by others. Think
of the Wind-God's daughter, whose husband imprisoned
                        her near
where the Iron Rocks guard the Bosporus.
Her young sons' stepmother gouged out their eyes, jealous.
(Enter blind Tiresias, led by a boy.)

TIRESIAS

Theban elders, observe how one can see
for two. I am blind, but a boy leads me.

CREON

Tiresias! What have you come to say,
old man?

TIRESIAS

                I will tell you, and you must pay
attention.

CREON

          I have always heard you out   710
and done as you advised. No need to doubt
that.

TIRESIAS

       Yes, and in so doing, you have steered
this state's ship straight, and each obstacle cleared.

CREON

       I know how much I owe you, Tiresias.

TIRESIAS

       Then listen to me when I tell you: as
a razor's edge is sharp, you stand now
on the perilous edge of the razor of Fate.

CREON

       Are you talking about our Theban state?
You have me worried—

TIRESIAS

                 You should be, you know.
For I was in the place of augury,   720
where all the birds of heaven find sanctuary,
when their beautiful songs were broken by a scream,
more screams, shrill cries, a strange, discordant dream
in which by slashing wings the air was stirred,
a whirlwind of wings, as every bird
turned on another, clawing with sharp talons,
tearing one another apart, and fell on
the living as on the dead.
              Shaken, I sought
benediction in a burnt offering, but
Hephaestus would not let the fire burn bright.   730
The thigh bones dripped a foul ooze—as if in fright—
which hissed and sputtered on the smoking ashes.

The gallbladder burst, blood and bile washing
out, and the raw fat melted, leaving bare
bone—and still the fire would not catch, flare,
burn. Creon, this is a sign the gods refuse
our offering. I bring you this bad news;
this is the sign I saw through my own seer.

And you, my king, are responsible for this state
of affairs, for the gods abominate   740
our shrines and altars that have now been stained
by the vomit of dogs and vultures, profaned
by Polynices' regurgitated corpse.
Glutted on blood, no birds can sing for us.

O son, this is serious! But remember:
All men make mistakes, but to make amends
is a kind of redemption, one that sends
a message of good will to all, somber
but full of hope. What point is there in killing
a man already dead? You must be willing   750
to change your mind. Take a prophet's advice—
free, though painfully gained from a failed sacrifice.

CREON

Advice? You so-called prophets are like archers,
letting your arrows fly at me! But what
you truly are, is confidence men,
trying to hustle me!
                              Leave me in peace.
Turn a *profit* somewhere else, old man,
speculate on the foreign exchange, wherever,
I don't care; but even if God's eagles
bore the body of Oedipus' son   760
to the heavens, morsel by rotting morsel,
I would not let you fool me into allowing his burial.
I know that no man can defile the gods.

I also know, Tiresias, that things
have come to a pretty sorry pass when
a soothsayer's soothsaying can be bought.

TIRESIAS

For God's sake, Creon, don't you—don't we all—
know—

CREON

Know what? What worn-out adage will you call
up next?

TIRESIAS

That the greatest wealth is wisdom.

CREON

Right. And its absence's worse than having no income   770
at all.

TIRESIAS

It's you who are bankrupt, Creon.

CREON

I will not trade insults with a mere peon,
even a prophet.

TIRESIAS

Yet you said my prophecies,
my well-meant warnings, are calculated lies.

CREON

Any man who reads palms hopes to have
his own palm crossed with silver.

TIRESIAS

And kings love
to cover themselves with ornaments of brass.

CREON

> Are you crazy? You think you can make an ass
> of me—? Just who do you think you're talking to?

TIRESIAS

> My king, of course—thanks to me, who helped you   780
> save the city.

CREON

>   I don't deny your knack
> for telling the future, but I think you lack
> the moral strength not to sell out your gift
> for gain, the will not to be swayed and drift
> into corruption.

TIRESIAS

>   Stop right there, or you
> will force me to reveal the dreadful truth
> of what I see in store for you.

CREON

>   Well, Sooth-
> sayer, spit it out. Just don't imagine
> you'll be paid for whatever wild tale you spin.

TIRESIAS

> There is no way you can redeem the future   790
> that I foretell for you.

CREON

>   Oh, of *that*, I'm sure,
> because nothing that you can say will buy
> me off, or change my mind. The girl will die!

TIRESIAS

> Then it is equally sure that you will pay
> for her life with the life of your own Hae-
> mon, your child for the child of Oedipus.

Because you have sentenced that child of light
to living death in an eternal night,
and insulted the gods of darkness by leaving
the dead, unsanctified, among the living,   800
usurping powers not even given to
the gods on high, the vengeful gods below
unleash their Furies to even the ghastly score.

Still think I have been bribed, Creon? Still think
I have sold out?

          It won't be long before
the sounds of lamentation will rise and sink
in the halls of your own house; while hateful
curses will be flung at you by all
abroad who left their brave sons at the gates
of Thebes, where the bodies lie in the open air,   810
to be interréd in a dog's throat, or to satiate
some circling vulture that carries the stench home.
                                 There,
they are preparing to move against you, Creon.

You said I was an archer. Very well.
These are my shafts, and they're aimed straight at you.
You can't duck them, nor is there anyone
to help you out, or save you from the hell
of self-reproach. You will feel the lasting sting
of every arrow.

          Now, boy, we'll leave the king
to take his rage out on somebody younger   820
than Tiresias. Maybe he'll get his tongue
back in his mouth, and therefore be more careful
about whom he chooses to call a lying fool.
(Exit Tiresias, led by boy.)

CHORAGOS
    The man is gone. But his forecast of sorrow
    haunts the present, and I have never, not

since I was young, known one of his prophecies
not to come true.

CREON

This is true.
                              Oh, God,
what should I do? How can I go back
on *my* word just because of his? Yet
I never meant to interfere with Fate.   830

CHORAGOS
Creon, listen to me.

CREON

                    What should I do?
Tell me. I'll do what you tell me to do!

CHORAGOS
Hurry, free Antigone from her tomb
and build another for dead Polynices.

CREON
You think this is what I should do?

CHORAGOS

                              Yes, Creon!
Hurry! The gods don't waste time debating
the merits and demerits of man's fate.

CREON
It's hard to swallow my pride, but I will.
Only an idiot tries to fight with Fate.

CHORAGOS
Do it yourself. Don't trust others. Go!   840

CREON

Yes, I will go.

You—servants—bring axes
to demolish the tomb. I buried her,
I will set her free myself.

Oh, hurry!
I am afraid—I should never have tried
to set myself above the laws of God.
What pride! What stupid, stupid pride! What pride!

(Creon rushes out, with servants.)

Praise and Plea

CHORUS

God, whose name is various and many
according to the manifold modes
of your being, son of the Almighty
and Semele—

Lord of the Mysteries   850
of Eleusis, where the sun goes down
behind green-black hills and the Ismenus,
her waters rippling like the limbs of maddened
Maenads, dances through the field—

God,
whose torches of lightning storm the mountains
and set the hearts and minds of your followers
aflame with ecstasy, so that they copy you,
wearing crowns of ivy and rioting
among the grapevines that grow along
the greening shore—

O God of Thebes, save us   860
from the sickness unto death that grips
us now, descend to us from Parnassus
or come swiftly across the sighing sea
to heal and save,

O God of the heavens,
of brilliant stars that throb like hearts, and of

the dark, irrational night, haunted by whispers,
come with the enraptured women who cry out
your constantly changing name, come, take us,
like them, in your arms, lead us in the dance
that is the dance of all that is,

save us.   870

(Enter a messenger, one of the servants who had left with Creon.)

MESSENGER

Listen to me, all of you who live
near here: A man's fortune is never fixed;
it changes constantly, and no one knows
what his fate will be. Consider Creon.
He seemed to have it all: military
triumph, a king's authority, a prince
of a son to crown his happiness. And now
it's all gone. He might as well be dead,
because a life without joy is no life
at all. He will be a walking dead man.   880
Oh, sure, he's still a rich man, with the perks
of a king, but without joy in life, power
and wealth are as worthless as the shadow of
a shade in Hades.

CHORAGOS

What bad news
do you bring?

MESSENGER

Both are dead, and the living
wish to be.

CHORAGOS

Who is dead? Who wants to die?
Speak up!

MESSENGER

Haemon is dead. He killed himself.

CHORAGOS
    But why?

MESSENGER
        Why? Because his own father
    had murdered Antigone.

CHORAGOS
                Tiresias,
    what you foretold has indeed come true!   890

MESSENGER
    This is what has happened. What you do
    about it is up to you.

CHORAGOS
                    Hold on, here comes
    the queen, Eurydice. Has she heard
    what has happened, or is she here by sheer
    coincidence?
(Enter Eurydice.)

EURYDICE
                I overheard you talking.
    I was leaving the palace to pray to Pallas
    when I heard what you were saying, and
    then I heard my own voice crying out
    and I fell back, fainting, in my handmaids' arms.
    The world went black. But let me know everything   900
    now: I'm used to tragedy and woe.

MESSENGER
    My queen, I was there, and I will tell you
    everything. I will not try to soften
    the truth, the hard truth, because to soften it
    would be to lie. The truth is always best.

I went with Creon to bury the corpse
of Polynices. We walked across the plain
to where it still lay. It had been dismembered
and eaten partially away by dogs.
We offered a prayer to the god of death   910
and to the dark night-goddess of crossroads
and graves, asking them to be merciful.
Then we sprinkled the corpse with holy water
and laid it on a bier of fresh-piled branches,
and lit the pyre. On the funeral urn
we heaped handfuls of his native land.
Then we hastened to the cold chamber of stone—
pitiless mockery of the bridal chamber—
in which Antigone would marry Death.
But the advance guard heard a cry come out   920
of the chamber, a cry that cut the sky
like a sword, and ran back to tell us,
and then, as we drew closer to the chamber,
Creon could hear for himself that hollow sound
of lamentation, so deep it seemed to come
from the time before language, and from Creon
himself there escaped a cry of such anguish
as would break your heart. "Oh God," he groaned aloud,
"am I a prophet too, to know this road
will be the darkest I have ever traveled?   930
That is my son's voice; it calls me on.
Hurry! Faster! Look into the tomb
through that crevice there and tell me if
it is Haemon's voice I hear, or if
I have gone mad."
                And so we looked, and saw
in the farthest corner of the dim cavern . . .
She had hanged herself. Fashioned a noose
of her linen veil. Haemon had his arms
around her waist, and was moaning, and holding
her to him, and saying that she was now   940
the bride of Death, that his father had stolen

her from him and, as in a stark parody
of the wedding that should have been, had given her hand
in marriage to cold-hearted death and the dark.

When Creon saw his son, he went toward him:
"My son," he begged, groaning, "what are you doing?
What impulse has seized you? Have you lost your mind?
Please, Haemon, come out of this place for the dead.
I beg you." But Haemon wouldn't listen.
He glared wildly at Creon and then, saying   950
nothing, he spat at him and drew his sword
and lunged. Creon shrank back and the sword missed him,
and Haemon, furious with himself for failing,
turned the sharp blade against himself and drove it
into his own side up to half its length,
and then, before he fell, he gathered the girl
in his arms, gently embracing her.
They lay together on the ground. Drawing
his last gasp of breath, he spewed blood
onto her pale cheek. It was so red   960
against the deathly whiteness of her cheek!
It seemed as if they shared a marriage bed,
there in that ruinous stone-cold house of the dead.
(Exit Eurydice, into the palace.)

CHORAGOS
    She's left without a word. I am afraid
    what this might mean.

MESSENGER
                    So am I. Let's hope
    it's because she's a private person who refuses
    to show her emotions in public.

CHORAGOS
                    That may be;
    but I am still troubled by her silence.

MESSENGER

Perhaps you're right. I should follow her
and make sure she doesn't do anything crazy.   970
(Exit Messenger. Enter Creon, accompanied by attendants, carrying
Haemon's body on a bier.)

CHORUS

The king is back!
                                    And in his arms he bears
the evidence convicting him of killing
his son.

CREON

                        I killed him. My own pride was the weapon
with which a father murdered his own son.

He was too young to die, but still he died
to pay for a foolish father's sin of pride.

CHORAGOS

This is true justice, but what a pity you've learned it
too late.

CREON

                        I have learned it in the school
of suffering. It is as if a god
singled me out and put his heavy hand   980
on my head, and under the weight of it
I went mad, became a barbarian,
a dumb savage, destroying what I loved
more than anything.
                                    I was determined
to feel this pain—hellbent on it.
(Enter Messenger.)

MESSENGER

                                            Sir,
there's yet another sorrow to be added

to the one you already carry in your arms
and heart; still more grief awaits you at home.

CREON

How could I feel more pain than I feel now?

MESSENGER

The mother of your dead son is dead,   990
Creon . . . Apparently it just happened—

CREON

Dead? My wife? I was already dead,
and now you take my life a second time!
Can this be true?

MESSENGER

You may see for yourself.
(The palace doors are opened to disclose the body of Eurydice.)

CREON

Oh God, it's true!—Death upon death upon—!
My son, and now my wife—! I cannot bear
any more grief; I tell you, my heart is breaking
apart—!

MESSENGER

Before the altar, your wife wept
for her lost sons, Megareus and Haemon,
and convicted their father of their deaths.   1000
And then she plunged a dagger into her heart,
and her eyes closed as if in sleep . . .

CREON

If only
I were dead too! I'm sick with fear—fear that
she is right. Will not someone kill me now?
I feel even now as if I'm dying of
grief, anguish, sorrow, dread of a life without love.

MESSENGER
> She charged you with her own death too, saying
> you caused it.

CREON
>   Oh, she was right, she was right!
> I alone am guilty, I do know it.
> I admit it. Lead me away. Let the world   1010
> forget I ever existed, for I have
> no kind of life now, no life worth living.

CHORAGOS
> Yes, take him away. It's best to take action
> immediately—if one can speak of anything
> being "good" at all, under the circumstances . . .

CREON
> May Fate move swiftly also, to ensure
> I will never see another sunrise,
> For that would be the best fate of all.

CHORAGOS *(gently)*
> We must leave the future to itself, Creon.
> There is enough to grieve for in the present.   1020

CREON
> I meant what I said with all my heart.

CHORAGOS
> But what we long for is beside the point:
> A man's fate is whatever it will be.

CREON
> Lead me away. I have been a foolish man.
> Never meaning to, I have murdered my son
> and my son's mother. There is nowhere I can turn,

no one to whom I can turn; they are dead.
All I touched as king has come to nothing.
My prideful self has been ground down to dust.
(Exit Creon with military attendants.)

CHORUS *(to the audience)*
    All our lives are in the hands of the gods.   1030
    If we would be content, we must be wise,
    and wisdom lies in obedience to the laws
    of the gods. Doubt not that if we doubt
    this, the gods will teach us otherwise.

Glossary

Abae (a'-bye). Town in Phocis where there was a temple and an oracle of Apollo.

Achaea (a-kye'-a). Region in the northeast Peloponnese.

Achelous (a-kel'-oh-us). God of the river of the same name in Epirus.

Acheron (ak'-er-on). River in Epirus which, because of its dead appearance, was said to be one of the rivers of hell.

Achilles (a-kil'-eez). Son of Peleus and Thetis, the best of the Greek warriors at Troy, and hero of the *Iliad*.

Adrastus (a-dras'-tus). King of Argos, one of the Seven against Thebes.

Aegean Sea. Part of the Mediterranean between Greece and Asia Minor.

Aegeus (ee-jee'-us). Son of Pandion and king of Athens. Father of Theseus by Aethra.

Aegisthus (ee-gis'-thus). Son of Thyestes, cousin of Agamemnon and Menelaus. Clytemnestra's lover.

Aenia (een'-i-a). City in Macedonia.

Aeolus (ee'-o-lus). God of the winds.

Aetolia (ee-tol'-i-a). Country in the middle of Greece of which Tydeus was king.

Agamemnon (ag-a-mem'-non). King of Mycenae, husband of Clytemnestra, and brother of Menelaus, king of Sparta. They were sons of Pleisthenes the son of Atreus (or, in some versions, they were themselves sons of Atreus).

Agenor (a-jee'-nor). King of Phoenicia, father of Cadmus and Europa.

Ajax (ay'-jaks). Son of Telamon king of Salamis and Eriboea, brother of Teucer. One of the great warriors at Troy.

Alcmene (alk-mee'-nee). Daughter of Electryon, mother of Heracles by Zeus, who appeared in her husband Amphitryon's shape.

Amphiaraus (am-fee-ar'-ee-us). One of the Seven against Thebes. Husband of Eriphyle, Adrastus' sister, father of Alcmaeon. Polynices bribed her with Harmonia's necklace to persuade Amphiaraus to participate in the war. Alcmaeon killed Eriphyle in revenge.

Amphitrite (am-fi-trye′-tee). Daughter of Oceanus and Tethis, wife of Poseidon, mother of Triton.

Antigone (an-ti′-go-nee). Daughter of Oedipus and Jocasta, sister of Eteocles, Polynices, and Ismene.

Antilochus (an-til′-o-kus). King of Messenia, son of Nestor.

Aphrodite (af-ro-dye′-tee). Latin Venus. Goddess of love.

Apollo (a-pol′-ow). God of music, healing, and prophecy. Son of Zeus and Leto, twin brother of Artemis.

Arcturus (ark-too′-rus). Star near the tail of Ursa Major that appears in October and portends great tempests.

Areopagus (air-ee-o-pay′-gus). The "hill of Ares," northwest of the Acropolis in Athens.

Ares (air′-ez). Latin Mars. God of war.

Argos (ar′-gos). (1) Strictly speaking, an ancient city, the capital of Argolis in the Peloponnese. But all the inhabitants of the Peloponnese, and even all the Greeks, are called Argives. (2) Son of Zeus for whom the city was named

Artemis (ar′-te-mis). Virgin goddess of the rural landscape and of hunting, prophecy, and childbirth. Daughter of Zeus and Leto, elder twin sister of Apollo.

Asclepius (es-klee′-pi-us). Son of Apollo, god of healing.

Atalanta (a-ta-lan′-ta). Virgin huntress, companion of Artemis. Promised to marry someone who could defeat her in a footrace. Mother of Parthenopaeus.

Athena (a-thee′-na). Latin Minerva. Goddess of wisdom and patroness of Athens.

Atreus (ay′-tree-us). Son of Pelops, father of Agamemnon and Menelaus, brother of Thyestes, whom he caused to eat the flesh of his own sons. (Or in some versions, he was the father of Pleisthenes and grandfather of Agamemnon and Menelaus.)

Atridae (a-trye′-dee). Agamemnon and Menelaus, the sons of Atreus, are often referred to as the Atridae; when this happens, the Greek uses "dual" forms for the verbs.

Aulis (owl′-is). Port in Boeotia where the Greek fleet gathered. The site of the sacrifice of Iphigenia.

Bacchantes (bak-kan'-teez). Also called Bacchae, the priestesses of Bacchus.

Bacchus (bak'-us). God of wine and drinking, son of Zeus and Semele. The Bacchanalia were his festivals.

Barca (bar'-ka). Town in Lydia.

Boeotia (bee-oh'-sha). District in eastern Greece.

Bosporus (bos'-por-us). Straits connecting the Black Sea and the Sea of Azov, center of a major kingdom.

Cadmus (kad'-mus). Son of Agenor and sister of Europa. He established the country called Boeotia and founded the city of Thebes, which he populated with men (Spartoi) who sprang from the teeth of a dragon he had killed. He married Harmonia, and introduced the alphabet into Greece.

Calchas, or sometimes Kalchas (kal'-kus). Soothsayer who accompanied the Greeks, and who told Agamemnon at Aulis that he must sacrifice his daughter Iphigenia.

Capaneus (ka-pa-nay'-us). One of the Seven against Thebes.

Cenaeum (se-nay'-um). Cape at Euboea.

Centaurs (sen'-taurz). Creatures who were half human and half horse; lived in Thessaly.

Cephallenia (sef-a-leen'-ya). An Ionian island.

Chiron (kye'-ron). Centaur who was wounded in the knee by a poisoned arrow of Heracles. The pain was so excruciating that he begged Zeus to deprive him of his immortality so he could die. He was placed among the constellations and became Sagittarius.

Chryse (kree'-say). Nymph who fell in love with Philoctetes and, when he rejected her, set a viper to bite him on the foot.

Chrysothemis (kri-so'-the-mis). One of the daughters of Agamemnon and Clytemnestra, sister of Orestes and Electra, and Iphigenia.

Cithaeron (ki-thy'-ron). Mountain in Boeotia sacred to Zeus and the Muses.

Clytemnestra (kly-tem-nes'-tra). Daughter of Leda, sister of Helen, wife of Agamemnon, mistress of Aegisthus, and mother of Iphigenia, Orestes, and Electra.

Colonus (ka-loh'-nus). Area in Attica north of Athens.

Corinth (kor'-inth). City of Greece on the Isthmus of Corinth.

Creon (kray'-on). Brother of Jocasta and king of Thebes after the death of Polynices and Eteocles.

Crete (kreet). Large Mediterranean island.

Crisa (kris'-a). Plain between Delphi and Corinth, sacred to Apollo.

Cronus (kro'-nus). Latin Saturn.Titan, son of Heaven (Uranus) and Earth (Gaia). He married his sister Rhea; their children included Demeter, Hades, Hera, Hestia, Poseidon, and Zeus, who overthrew him.

Cyllene (sy-lee'-nee). Mountain in Arcadia, and the town on its slope.

Cyprus (sye'-prus). Large Mediterranean island, birthplace of Aphrodite.

Danaë (da'-nah-ay). Daughter of Acrisius king of Argos and Eurydice. Acrisius imprisoned her, Zeus visited her in a shower of gold, and Danaë gave birth to Perseus. Acrisius set them adrift in a chest, but they landed safely on the island of Seriphus.

Daphne (daf'-nee). Virgin huntress, daughter of a river god. Attempted to avoid rape by Apollo but couldn't outrun him, so prayed to either her father or Zeus, who turned her into a bay tree.

Daulis (dow'-lis). Town in Phocis where Philomela and Procne made Tereus eat the flesh of his son.

Daughters of Earth. Name for the Eumenides.

Deianira (day-a-nye'-ra). Daughter of Oeneus and Althaea, sister of Meleager, wife of Heracles.

Delos (del'-os). Small island, birthplace of Apollo and Artemis.

Delphi (del'-fye). Town on the southwest side of Mount Parnassus where the Pythia gave oracular messages inspired by Apollo.

Demeter (de-meet'-er). Latin Ceres. Earth-mother goddess of grains and harvests, mother of Persephone.

Diomedes (dy-o-mee'-deez). Warrior, son of Tydeus and Deiphyle daughter of Adrastus.

Dionysus (dye-o-nee'-sus). Another name for Bacchus. The Dionysia was the wine festival in the god's honor.

Dirce (dir'-see). (1) Second wife of Lycus, king of Thebes. He married her after divorcing Antiope. After the divorce, Antiope became pregnant by Zeus, and Dirce, suspecting Lycus was the father, imprisoned and tormented Antiope, who nonetheless escaped and bore Amphion and Zethus on Mount Cithaeron. (2) Spring or river at Thebes named for her.

Dodona (do-doh'-na). Town in Epirus (some say Thessaly) where there was a temple to Zeus and the most ancient oracle of Greece. There was a grove of sacred oak trees surrounding the temple.

Dorians (dor'-i-anz). Race of people who invaded and settled in Greece in the twelfth century B.C.

Echidna (ek-id'-na). Monster the upper part of whose body is that of a beautiful woman and the lower part that of a serpent.

Electra (e-lek'-tra). Daughter of Agamemnon and Clytemnestra, sister of Orestes, Iphigenia, and Chrysothemis.

Eleusis (el-oo'-sis). Town near Athens where there was a religious festival celebrated every fifth year.

Epigoni (ep-i-goh'-nee). Name for Eteocles and Polynices.

Eriboea (er-i-bee'-a). Wife of Telamon and the mother of Ajax.

Erinyes (er-in'-yees). The Furies, the spirits of divine vengeance, who later become the Eumenides.

Erymanthus (er-i-man'-thus). Arcadian mountan, also a river and a town.

Eteocles (e-tee'-o-cleez). Son of Oedipus and Jocasta, brother of Polynices.

Eteoclus (e-tee-oh'-clus). Son of Iphis, one of the Seven against Thebes.

Euboea (you-bee'-a). The long island that stretches from the Gulf of Pagasae to Andros, the chief cities of which were Chalcis and Eretria.

Eumenides (you-men'-i-deez). The Furies in their benevolent aspect.

Europa (you-roh'-pa). Daughter of Agenor king of Phoenicia, mother of Minos, Rhadamanthus, and Sarpedon by Zeus, who in the form of a bull carried her off.

Eurydice (you-rid'-i-see). (1) Wife of Creon, mother of Haemon. (2) Wife of the singer Orpheus, brought back from Hades.

Eurysaces (you-ris-ak'-eez). Son of Ajax and Tecmessa.

Eurystheus (you-ris'-thee-us). Son of Sthenelus and Nicippe; Hera hastened his birth so that Heracles would have to be his servant. He was the one who ordered Heracles to perform his famous twelve labors.

Eurytus (you'-ri-tus). King of Oechalia, father of Iole.

Evenus (ev-ee'-nus). Son of Ares, father of Marpessa, whose virginity he protected by requiring her suitors to compete with him in chariot races. When Idas eloped with Marpessa, Evenus gave chase, but could not overtake the fleeing pair. He killed his horses and drowned himself in the Lycormas river, which was thereafter known as the Evenus.

Furies. See Erinyes.

Hades (hay'-deez). Latin Pluto.The world of the dead, or the god who ruled it.

Haemon (hy'-mon). Son of Creon king of Thebes and Eurydice. Killed himself on discovering Antigone's suicide.

Hector. Son of Priam and Hecuba, and the chief warrior of Troy. He married Andromache.

Helen. Daughter of Leda, sister of Clytemnestra, wife of Menelaus, taken by Paris to Troy.

Helenus (hel'-en-us). Son of Priam and Hecuba, a soothsayer. He married Andromache, widow of his brother Hector.

Helicon (hel'-i-kon). Mountain in southwest Boeotia sacred to the Muses.

Hephaestus (hef-fes'-tus). Latin Vulcan. God of fire and smithing.

Hera (her'-a). Latin Juno. Wife and sister of Zeus, and queen of heaven.

Heracles (her'-a-kleez). Latin Hercules. Son of Zeus by Alcmene, husband of Deianira. He was tormented by Hera and made to perform many arduous labors.

Hermeaum (her-may'-um). Town of Arcadia.

Hermes (her'-meez). Latin Mercury. Son of Zeus and Maia. He was the messenger god and patron of messengers and merchants.

Hippodamia (hip-o-dam'-i-a). Daughter of Oenomaus of Pisa, who refused to let her marry unless her suitor could defeat him in a chariot race. Those who lost had to forfeit their lives. Thirteen such suitors had perished when Pelops appeared, bribed Myrtilius, Oenomaus. charioteer, and thus contrived to win her.

Hippomedon (hip-pom'-e-don). Son of Talus, one of the Seven against Thebes.

Hydra. Monster that lived in Lake Lerna in the Peloponnese. It had a hundred heads, and as soon as one was cut off, two more grew from the wound. Heracles nonetheless killed it.

Hyllus (hill'-us). Son of Heracles and Deianira.

Ilium (il'-i-um) or Ilion. Name for Troy.

Io (eye'-oh). Daughter of the river Inachus, raped and turned into a white cow by Zeus. Tormented by a gadfly sent by Hera, she wandered all over the world until Zeus restored her.

Iole (eye'o-lay). Daughter of Eurytus, captive of Heracles.

Iphigenia (if-i-jin-eye'-a). Daughter of Agamemnon and Clytemnestra whom he sacrificed at Aulis.

Iphitus (if-it'-tus), Son of Eurytus whom Heracles killed.

Iron Rocks. The Symplegades.

Ismene (iz-may'-nay). Sister of Antigone, Polynices, and Eteocles.

Ismenus (iz-may'-nus). River near Eleusis.

Ithaca. Island off the western coast of Greece of which Odysseus was king.

Itys (it'-is). Son of Tereus, king of Thrace, and Procne, who was killed by his mother and served up as meat for his father. He was changed into a pheasant, his mother into a nightingale, and his father into an owl or hoopoe.

Jocasta (jo-kas'-ta). Wife of Laius, mother and wife of Oedipus.

Labdacus (lab'-da-cus). Father of Laius who was father of Oedipus.

Labdacidae (lab-da'-ki-dye). The descendants of Labdacus.

Laertes (lay-air'-tees). Father of Odysseus.

Laius (lay-us). Son of Labdacus, father of Oedipus.

Laomedon (lay-ah'-me-don). King of Troy, father of Priam.

Lemnos (lem'-nos). Island in the Aegean sacred to Hephaestus, now called Stalimine.

Lerna. Lake where the Hydra lived.

Libya. Pretty much all of Africa except for Egypt.

Lichas (lik'-as). Herald of Heracles

Locris (lok'-ris). Region of Greece north of the bay of Corinth.

Loxias (lok'-see-us). Name for Apollo.

Lycia (li'-si-a). Country of Asia Minor.

Lycomedes (ly-kom'-e-deez). King of Scyros, the island on which Achilles hid among the women to avoid service in the Trojan war. His daughter, Deidamia, married Achilles and bore Neoptolemus.

Lydia (li'-di-a). Kingdom of Asia Minor; Croesus was its king.

Maenads (mee'-nads). The Bacchantes.

Magnesia. Town of Asia Minor on the Meander river, a few miles from Ephesus.

Maia (mye'-a). Daughter of Atlas and one of the Pleiades, mother of Hermes by Zeus.

Malis (ma'-lis). One of Omphale's women servants whom Heracles loved.

Menelaus (me-ne-lay'-us). King of Sparta, son of Atreus, brother of Agamemnon, husband of Helen.

Menoeceus (men-ee'-kee-us). Descendant of Echion, father of Creon and Jocasta.

Merope (meh'-o-pay). Wife of Polybus king of Corinth, adopted Oedipus.

Mycenae (my-see'-nee). Town in the Peloponnese where Agamemnon ruled.

Myrtilus (mir-til'-us). Charioteer to Oenomaus (q.v.).

Mysia (miz'-i-a). Country of Asia Minor adjoining Phrygia.

Nemea (neem'-i-a). Town of Argolis near the wood where Heracles killed the lion.

Nemesis (nem'-e-sis). Goddess of divine vengeance, daughter of Oceanus.

Neoptolemus (ne-op-tol'-e-mus). Son of Achilles and Deidamia, also called Pyrrhus (yellow) because of the color of his hair.

Nessus (nes'-us). Centaur who tried to rape Deianira. Heracles shot him with a poisoned arrow. Nessus as he died gave his cloak to Deianira, telling her it would restore a lover's interest. Actually, it was deadly poison and, when Deianira used it, it killed Heracles.

Nestor (nes'-tor). Son of Neleus and Chloris, companion of Menelaus.

Niobe (ny'-o-bee). Daughter of Tantalus, wife of Amphion of Thebes. She boasted that she was superior to Leto because of her many children, whereupon Leto's children Apollo and Artemis killed Niobe's children. She returned to Lydia, her native land, and was transformed to stone from which tears flowed continually.

Odysseus (o-dis'-yus). Latin Ulysses. King of Ithaca and one of the Greek heroes of the Trojan war. His domestic situation with faithful Penelope awaiting his return is often contrasted with Agamemnon's difficulties.

Oechalia (ee-kal'-i-a). Region and town in the Peloponnese of which Eurytus was king. It was destroyed by Heracles.

Oedipus (ed'-i-pus). Son of Laius and Jocasta, husband of Jocasta, father of Antigone, Ismene, Polynices, and Eteocles.

Oeneus (ee'-nee-us). (1) King of Calydon, father by Althaea of Meleager and Deianira. (2) Father of Tydeus.

Oenomaus (ee-no-mah'-us). King of Pisa (the area around Olympia), father of Hippodamia, whom he promised to whoever could defeat him in a chariot race. Pelops did so by trickery.

Oeta (eet'-a). Mountain between Thessaly and Macedonia on which Heracles died.

Olympia (o-lim'-pi-a). Sanctuary of Zeus by the river Alphaeus.

Olympus (o-lim'-pus). Mountain in Thessaly so tall that the Greeks believed it touched the heavens; it was therefore the home of the Olympian gods.

Omphale (om-fal'-ay). Queen of Lydia to whom Hermes sells Heracles as a slave.

Orestes (or-es'-teez). Son of Agamemnon and Clytemnestra, brother of Electra, Iphigenia, and Chrysothemis. Married Hermione.

Ortygia (or-ti'-jee-a). Ancient name for Delos, birthplace of Artemis and Apollo.

Pactolus (pak'-to-lus). Lydian river rising on Mount Tmolus.

Pallas (pal'-las). Name for Athena.

Pan. God of shepherds and hunters. He had horns and goat feet and invented the syrinx or reed flute.

Paris. Son of Priam and Hecuba who abducted Helen from Sparta.

Parnassus (par-nas'-us). Mountain in Phocis, sacred to the Muses.

Parthenopaeus (par-then-o-pye'-us). Son of Atalanta, one of the Seven against Thebes.

Patroclus (pat-rok'-lus). Greek warrior who was Achilles' close friend.

Pelops (pel'-ops). Son of Tantalus, who cut him up and served him to the Phrygian gods. Restored to life, he obtained Hippodamia after defeating Oenomaus in a chariot race by trickery. Father of Atreus.

Peparethos (pep-ar-eth'-us). Island in the Aegean off the Macedonian coast.

Persephone (per-sef'-o-nee). Latin Proserpine. Daughter of Demeter and queen of Hades.

Phanoteus (fan-oh'-te-us). Uncle of Strophius who was said to have fought with his brother Crisus in the womb. Crisus was Strophius' father and Pylades' grandfather. Orestes claims to be Phanoteus' messenger.

Phasis (fa'-sis). River in Calchis that flows into the Black Sea.

Philoctetes (fil-ok-tee'-teez). Son of Poeas and Demonassa, one of the Argonauts, who is was put ashore on the island of Chryse because of the foul smelling wound to his foot.

Phocis (foh'-kis). District of Greece next to Boeotia on the Gulf of Corinth.

Phoebus (fee'-bus). Name for Apollo.

Phoenix (fee'-nix). Son of Amyntor, king of Argos, who was tutor to Achilles and foster father of Achilles' son Neoptolemus.

Phrygia (fri'-jee-a). Country in Asia Minor.

Pirithous (pir-i'-thoo-us). Lapith, son of Zeus and Ixion's wife Dia, friend of Theseus.

Pleuron (plow'-ron). Land where Oeneus ruled and from which his daughter Deianira came.

Poeas (pee'-as). Father of Philoctetes.

Polybus (pol'-i-bus). King of Corinth. He and his wife Merope, childless, adopted the infant Oedipus.

Polydorus (po-li-dor'-us). Youngest son of Priam and Hecuba, killed by his brother-in-law Polymestor.

Polynices (po-lee-nye'-seez). Son of Oedipus and Jocasta, brother of Eteocles, Antigone, and Ismene.

Poseidon (po-sye'-don). Latin Neptune. God of the sea, brother of Demeter, Hades, Hera, Hestia, and Zeus.

Priam (prye'-am). King of Troy, son of Laomedon.

Procne (prok'-ne). Daughter of Pandion, sister of Philomela. Her husband Tereus raped Philomela and cut out her tongue to guarantee her silence, but she wove the story into a piece of cloth and sent it to Procne. In revenge, Procne killed her son Itys and served him to Tereus.

Prometheus (pro-mee'-thee-us). Son of the Titan Iapetus and the Oceanid Clymene. Stole fire from the gods, punished and imprisoned, eventually freed by Heracles.

Pylades (pye'-la-deez). Son of Strophius, companion and cousin of Orestes.

Pythia (pith'-ee-a). Oracle of Apollo at Delphi, which was the site of the Pythian games.

Pytho (pye'-tho). Ancient name of Delphi, so-called because of the great serpent Apollo killed there.

Salamis (sal'-a-mis). Island in the Saronic Gulf off Eleusis.

Scamander (ska-man'-der). River near Troy.

Scyros (skee'-ros). Island off Euboea.

Semele (sem'-e-le). Daughter of Cadmus and Harmonia, and, by Zeus, the mother of Bacchus.

Sicily. Large island in the Mediterranean.

Sigeum (si-gay'-um). A town of the Troad on the promontory of the same name where the Scamander meets the sea.

Sisyphus (si'-si-fus). Son of Aeolus, king of Corinth. Tried to cheat Death, condemned in Hades endlessly to roll a huge stone up a mountain.

Spercheus (sper'-kee-os). River of Thessaly arising on mount Oeta.

Sphinx. Monster, part animal, part human, challenged by Odysseus.

Strophius (stro'-fee-us). King of Phocis, brother-in-law of Agamemnon, and father of Pylades.

Symplegades (sim-pleg'-a-deez). Wandering rocks that smashed together and prevented ships from passing through the Bosporus.

Talaus (Ta'-la-us). Father of Hippomedon.

Tantalus (tan'-ta-lus). King of Phrygia, son of Zeus, father of Pelops and Niobe.

Tecmessa (tek-mess'-a). Daughter of Teleutas, killed by Ajax, whose property she became and to whom she bore Eurysaces.

Telamon (tel'-a-mon). King of Salamis, comrade of Heracles, father of Ajax and Teucer.

Teleutas (tel-oo'-tas). Father of Tecmessa.

Teucer (too'-ser). Son of Telamon king of Salamis, by Hesione.

Thebes (theebz). City in Boeotia.

Themis. Daughter of Uranus and Gaia who married Zeus and was the mother of the Horae (the Hours)—Diké (justice), Eirene (peace), Eunomia (good order)—and the Moirae (the Fates).

Thermopylae (ther-mop'-i-lee). Literally, the hot gates, the narrow pass that leads from Thessaly into Locris and Phocis. It is best known for the battle fought there in 480 B.C. between the Greeks and the Persians.

Thersites (ther-see'-teez). Foul-mouthed Greek warrior whom Achilles killed.

Theseus (thee'-see-us). Son of Aegeus and Aethra, king of Athens.

Thessaly. Territory to the north of Greece proper.

Thorician Rock. Monument at Colonus to the town of Thoricus, one of the twelve independent cities of Attica unified by Theseus.

Thrace (thrays). Area encompassing most of the world north of the Black Sea.

Tilphussa (til-fus'-a). Spring on Mt. Helicon where Tiresias died.

Tiresias (ti-rees'-i-us). Great prophet of Thebes who was turned into a woman and then back to a man. He was blinded, either by Athena because he caught sight of her bathing or by Hera because he said women had more pleasure in sex than men.

Tiryns (teer'-inz). Town in the Peloponnese founded by Tiryns, son of Argos. It was Heracles' home.

Trachis (tray'-kis). Town on the bay of Malea, near mount Oeta.

Tydeus (tid'-ee-us). One of the Seven against Thebes, father of Diomedes.

Wind God. Name for Aeolus.

Zeus (zoos). Latin Jupiter. Son of the Titans Cronus and Rhea, brother of Demeter, Hades, Hera (whom he married), Hestia, and Poseidon. After he overthrew Cronus he became the chief Greek god.

About the Translators

KELLY CHERRY is the author of more than a dozen books, including five volumes of poetry (most recently *Death and Transfiguration*), five novels (most recently *My Life and Dr. Joyce Brothers*), a collection of essays (*Writing the World*), and an autobiographical narrative (*The Exiled Heart*). Over 400 of her poems have appeared in such journals as the *Atlantic*, *American Scholar*, and *Georgia Review*, and some have been translated into Latvian, Chinese, and Czech. She is the recipient of a National Endowment for the Arts fellowship, a Romnes fellowship, a fellowship from the Wisconsin Arts Board, and, in 1990, the first James G. Hanes Poetry Prize of the Fellowship of Southern Writers, given in recognition of a distinguished body of work. She has been a Bread Loaf fellow and a Yaddo fellow. She has taught at the University of Wisconsin, Madison since 1977, since 1993 as the Evjue-Bascom Professor in the Humanities.

GEORGE GARRETT is the author of more than twenty-five books of poetry, fiction, drama, and criticism, and is the editor or coeditor of seventeen others. Among his recent books are *Days of Our Lives Lie in Fragments: New and Old Poems, 1957–1997*, *The King of Babylon Shall Not Come Against You*, *The Sorrows of Fat City*, *Whistling in the Dark*, and *The Old Army Game*. He has served as editor or coeditor of several literary magazines and is currently fiction editor for *Texas Review*. He has been a recipient of a Guggenheim fellowship, a National Endowment for the Arts sabbatical fellowship, a Ford Foundation grant, and the Rome Prize of the American Academy of Arts and Letters. He was awarded a Literary Lion citation from the New York Public Library and is Cultural Laureate of the Commonwealth of Virginia. He received the T. S. Eliot award in 1989 and, more recently, the PEN/Faulkner Bernard Malamud Award for Short Fiction. He has taught at the University of Michigan, Bennington College, Princeton University, and elsewhere. He is the Henry Hoyns Professor of

Creative Writing at the University of Virginia and Chancellor of the Fellow-ship of Southern Writers.

JASCHA KESSLER has published five fiction collections, in-cluding *Siren Songs & Classical Illusions*, and three poetry volumes, includ-ing *In Memory of the Future*, and has written several plays and *The Cave*, a libretto for a full-length opera with a score by Ned Rorem. He was the first American writer to be honored with the Hungarian PEN Club's Memorial Medal for his collaborative translation projects in fiction and verse and has won the Translation Center's George Soros Foundation Prize for *Catullan Games*, a volume of poems from the Hungarian of Sándor Rákos. He has received a Major Hopwood Award for Poetry, a National Endowment for the Arts fellowship, two Senior Fulbright awards, a California Arts Council fellowship, and a Rockefeller Foundation fellowship. His literary essays have appeared widely. Since 1961 he has been Professor of English and Modern Literature at the University of California, Los Angeles.